SCOTS
IN THE
USA AND CANADA
1825 - 1875

PART SEVEN

by
David Dobson

CLEARFIELD

Copyright © 2025
by David Dobson
All Rights Reserved

Published for Clearfield Company by
Genealogical Publishing Company
Baltimore, Maryland
2025

ISBN: 9780806359779

INTRODUCTION

SCOTS IN THE USA AND CANADA, 1825-1875, PART SEVEN

Emigration from Scotland to the United States and Canada during the nineteenth century was significant both in absolute and relative terms. The mass movement that occurred was a continuation of a process that had its roots in the seventeenth century. What made Scottish emigrants different from most European emigrants of the Victorian period was the fact that they generally had industrial and commercial skills that were in demand at home, and were not of the rural worker surplus forced off the land. There were notable exceptions to this generalisation, particularly those who emigrated as a result of the Highland Clearances, some of whom are listed in this book. Most Scottish emigrants of the period, however, were skilled, educated workers from urban backgrounds whose expertise was in great demand in the rapidly industrializing cities of North America. The level of annual emigration varied, reflecting the fluctuations of the trade cycle during the century.

This volume is largely based on contemporary newspapers, such as the "Aberdeen Journal", monumental inscription lists, university records, and government records located in archives. Notably, these include the National Records of Scotland and the National Library of Scotland, both in Edinburgh, that contained the Registers of Sasines which records property transactions; and the Services of Heirs, which records the change of ownership of property on the death of an individual. This volume also includes some emigrant ship lists. In addition to the data of the nineteenth century, I have included a small **Addendum** (beginning on page 111) of emigrant references dating from the seventeenth and eighteenth centuries, too few to form a separate book but too valuable to ignore.

David Dobson
Dundee, Scotland, 2025

REFERENCES

AJ Aberdeen Journal, series

AUL Aberdeen University Library

BM Book of Mackay, [Edinburgh, 1896]

BM Blackwood's Magazine, seris

CM Caledonian Mercury, series

DAC Dumfries Archive Centre

DCA Dundee City Archives

DCB Dictionary of Canadian Biography

DJ Dunfermline Journal, series

DUA Dundee University Archives

EAR Edinburgh Academy Register

EEC Edinburgh Evening Courant, series

EFR East Fife Record, series

EMG Edinburgh Medical Graduates

EMR Edinburgh Marriage Register

F. Fasti Ecclesiae Scoticanie, [Edinburgh, 1915]

FFP Fife Free Pres, series

FH Fife Herald, series

FJ Fife Journal, series

FMS/NC Federal Mortality Schedule, North Carolina

GCA Glasgow City Archives

GM Gentleman's Magazine, series

HBCA Hudson Bay Company Archives, Winnipeg

HCA Highland Council Archives, Inverness

HS History Scotland, series

JGJ John O'Groats Journal, series

KCA King's College Archives, Aberdeen

LAC Libraries and Archives Canada

MAGU Matriculation Albums of Glasgow University

MCA Marischal College Archives, Aberdeen

MU Memorial University, Newfoundland

NARA National Archives, Records Administration

NLS National Library of Scotland

NRAS National Register of Archives, Scotland

NRS National Records of Scotland

OA Orkney Archives

PANB Public Archives of New Brunswick

PJ People's Journal, series

RGG Register of Glasgow Graduates

RGS Register of the Great Seal of Scotland

RSSP Recovering Scotland's Slavery Past, [Edinburgh,2015]

S The Scotsman, series

SAU St Andrews University

SG Scottish Guardian, series

S/H Services of Heirs

SRA Strathclyde Regional Archives

SS Surnames of Scotland, [New York, 1946]128

OA Orkney Archives

TNA The National Archives, London

TGSI Transactions of the Gaelic Society of Inverness, series.

TNA The National Archives, Kew

RGG Register of Glasgow Graduates

UA University of Aberdeen

WAJ The Wreck of the Annie Jane, [Stornaway 2017]

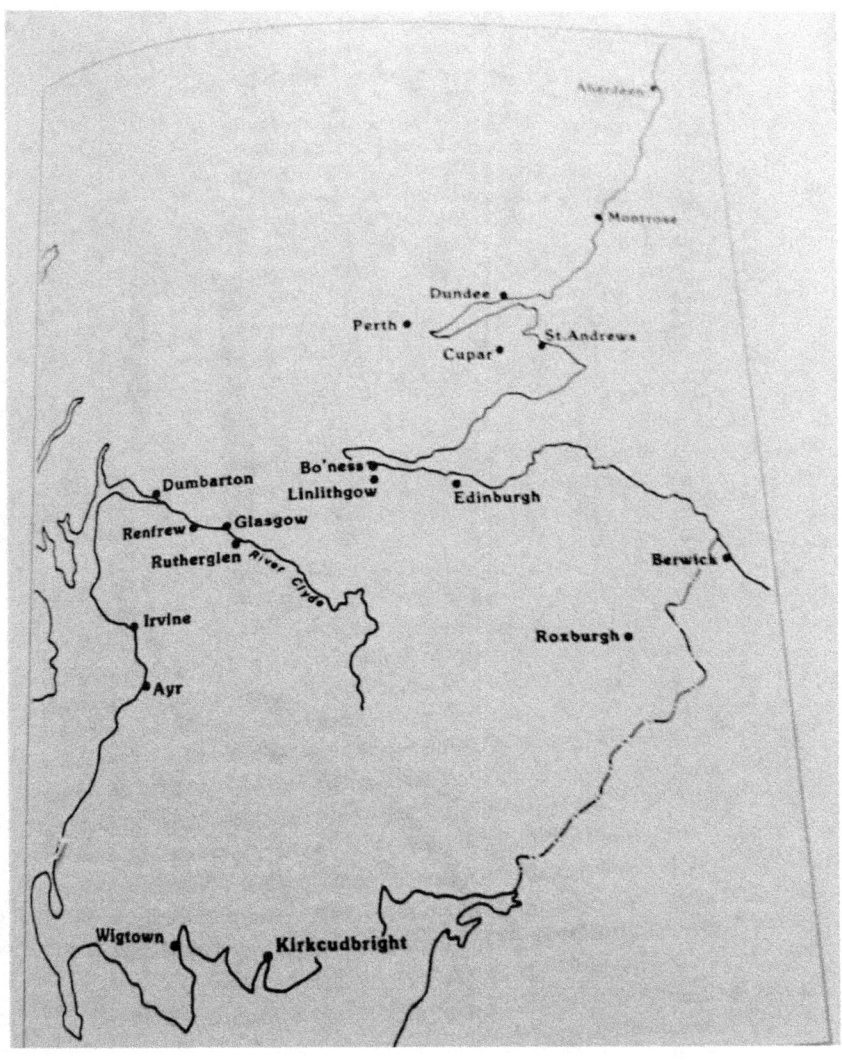

Map of central Scotland, showing location of Glasgow.

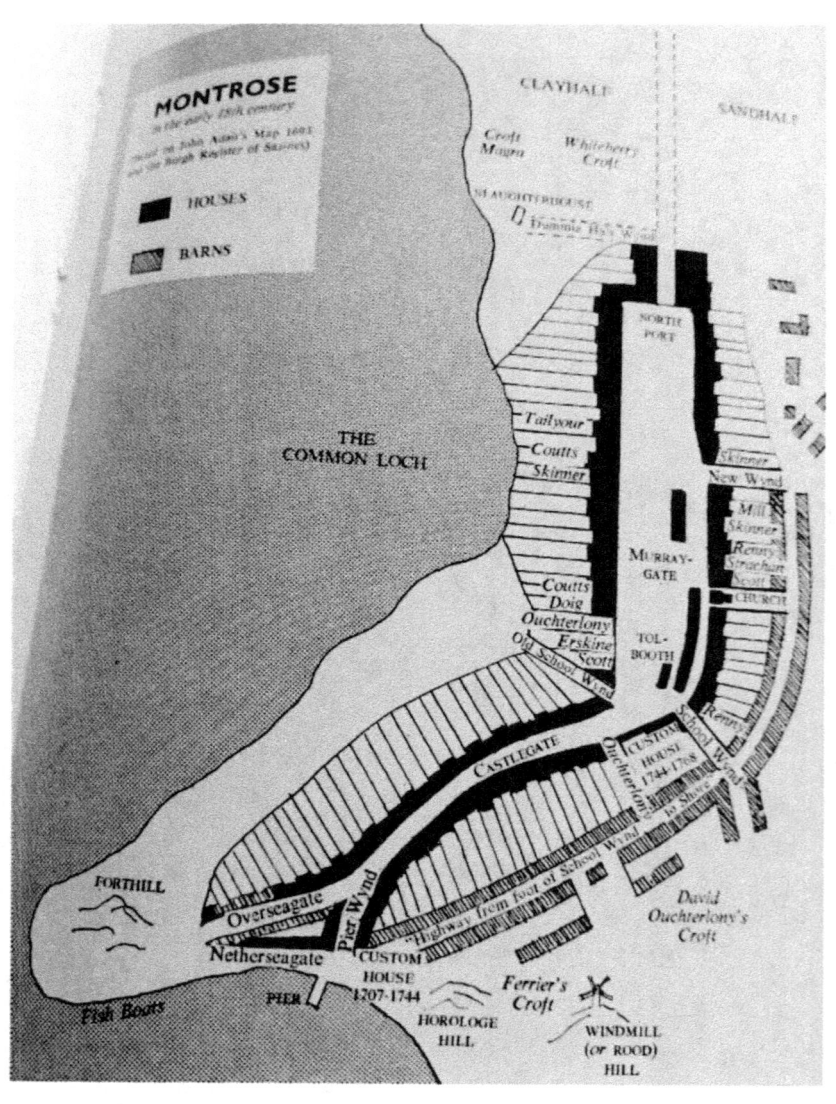

Map of Montrose in the early 18th century, based on John Adair's map of 1693 and the Burgh Register of Sasines.

Montrose harbor and the Horologe Hill, painted by Henrietta Ouchterlony in 1810.

New Amsterdam, an early sketch.

Halifax, Nova Scotia, 1764

ABEL, WILLIAM, born 1788, a merchant tailor from Easter Carnie, Skene, Aberdeenshire, died at Simcoe, Canada West, on 31 August 1865. [AJ.27.9.1865]

ABERDEIN, ANDREW, born 1833 in Downiehills, Peterhead, Aberdeenshire, a carpenter, died at St Martin's, Lower Canada, on 24 February 1858. [AJ]

ADAMS, GILBERT, born in Louisville, Kentucky, graduated MD from Glasgow University in 1853. [RGG]

ADAM, JAMES, in Cambridge, USA, heir to his grandmother Mary Robertson, wife of John Galt a mason in Govan, Glasgow, who died on 23 November 1859 in New Brunswick. [NRS.S/H.1900]

ADAMS, FORDYCE, daughter of Francis Adams, a chartered accountant in Montreal, Quebec, died in Kingston, Canada West, on 18 December 1865. [Banchory Ternan gravestone, Aberdeenshire]

ADAMS, JESSIE FORDYCE, daughter of Fra, [Banchory Ternan gravestone, Aberdeenshire]

ADAMSON, THOMAS, from Halbeath in Fife, died in St Mary's, Elk County, Pennsylvania, on 30 June 1883. [DJ]

AIKMAN, JOHN, in New York, a deed with John Bryce, 10 June 1828. [NRS.RD435.207]

AITCHISON, JAMES, son of William Aitchison a brewer in Edinburgh, in Tilbury, Lower Canada, and later in London, Upper Canada, a letter in 1837. [NRS.GD1.92.18]

AITKEN, ISABELLA, daughter of Reverend Roger Aitken in Nova Scotia, late of Aberdeen, died in Fredericton, New Brunswick on 14 January 1848. [AJ]

AITKEN, THOMAS, born 1799 in Bo'ness, West Lothian, graduated MA from Glasgow University in 1818, rector of Halifax Academy, Nova Scotia, in 1828 and a missionary there. [F.7.613]

AITKEN, WILLIAM, born 1880 son of William Aitken and his wife Helen, died at 506 West 12th Street, New York, on 23 May 1885. [S.13086]

AITKEN, WILLIAM, in New York, was served heir to his father Andrew Aitken, an ironmonger in Airdrie, Lanarkshire, who died on 31 August 1897. [NRS.S/H]

ALEXANDER, ANDREW SNODGRASS MUIR, in Chicago, Illinois, heir to his uncle George Lewis William Forbes, a solicitor in Banff, who died on 4 January 1862, re property in Fordyce, Moray, 4 February 1889. [NRS.S/H]

ALEXANDER, GEORGE, in Halifax, Nova Scotia, an inventory, 1871, [NRS.SC70.156.494]

ALLAN, ALEXANDER, late advocate in Aberdeen, died in Preston, Canada West on 15 July 1855. [AJ]

ALLAN, Mrs ANN DUNCAN or, born 1833, died on 9 August 1877, Paris, Brant, Ontario, an inventory, 1877. [NRS.SC70.186.544] [AJ.4.9.1877]

ALLAN, Mrs CHRISTIAN, born 1757, daughter of John Dyce in Tillygreig, Aberdeenshire, died in St John's, New Brunswick, on 19 June 1844. [AJ]

ALLAN, DAVID, born 1852, son of Wilson Allan in Dunfermline, died in Montreal on 9 April 1854. [DJ]

ALLEN, JOHN, of Toronto, Ontario, graduated CM from Glasgow University in 1835. [RGG]

ALLAN, JOHN B., a silverware manufacturer in Chicago son of William Allan a merchant in Morningside, Edinburgh, married Jeanette Martin West, daughter of Hugh Watt in Chicago, formerly in Midlothian, in Chicago on 20 January 1898. [S.17040]

ALLAN, WILLIAM, born 1842 in Kilconquhar, Fife, son of George Allan a currier, died in Brooklyn, New York, on 28 July 1910. [EFR]

ALLAN, Dr WILLIAM, in Ontario, a deed dated 1882. [NRS,RD1854.259.97]

ALLARDYCE, ROBERT ALEXANDER, in Amboy, Illinois, heir to his father Robert Alexander, a merchant in Calcutta, India, who died 24 June 1869, and to land in Fife. [NRS.S/H]

ALMON, WILLIAM BRUCE, from America, graduated MD from Edinburgh University in 1809. [EMG]

ALMON, WILLIAM JOHNSTON, from Nova Scotia, graduated MD from Glasgow University in 1838. [RGG]

ANDERSON, ALEXANDER, settled in Reach, Ontario, by 1848, a petitioner. [NRS.GD112.61.5]

ANDERSON, ANDREW, in Beckwith, Canada, in 1831. [NRS.SC.Perth.29.158]

ANDERSON, or BROWN, ANN WHITE, in Morristown, New York, heir to her father David Anderson in Arbroath, Angus, who died on 8 October 1886. [NRS.S/H]

ANDERSON, DUNCAN, settled in Reach, Ontario, by 1848, a petitioner. [NRS.GD112.61.5]

ANDERSON, GEORGE P., died in Denver, Colorado, on 11 October 1894, husband of Lizzie Hendrie, late of Aberdeen. [AJ]

ANDERSON, GEORGE, at Medical Lake, Washington, USA, was served heir to his mother Elizabeth Carnegy or Anderson in Little Brechin, Angus, who died on 16 March 1898. [NRS.S/H]

ANDERSON, JAMES, a merchant in Sydney, Cape Breton, Nova Scotia, accounts re the St Andrew of Aberdeen, master William Penn, 1842. [AUL.2295/1-2]

ANDERSON, JAMES, was ordained in 1865, a minister at Wallace and Pugwash, Nova Scotia, from 1866 until 1872, then at St James's, Newcastle, New Brunswick, from 1873 until 1880. [F.7.608]

ANDERSON, JAMES A., an architect in Detroit, Michigan, in 1878. [NRS.SCPerth.78.171]

ANDERSON, JANE, daughter of James Anderson in Edinburgh, died in Dartmouth, Halifax, Nova Scotia, on 14 September 1884, [S.12864]

ANDERSON, JESSIE ELDER, elder daughter of James Anderson, late of Townhead in Dolphintown, and Broomhills in Edinburgh, died on Kennedy Farm in Ohio on 31 January 1885. [S.12991]

ANDERSON, LOUIS P., in Victoria, Kansas, discharged his father's trustees, a deed in 1882. [NRS.RD1880.340.300]

ANDERSON, PETER, settled in Reach, Ontario, by 1848, a petitioner. [NRS.GD112.61.5]

ANDERSON, ROBERT, in Sydney, Nova Scotia, an inventory dated 1871. [NRS.SC70.151.353]

ANDERSON, VIOLET ALEXANDRA, in Clymer, Oregon, heir to her great-grandmother Isobel Noble, widow of Alexander Anderson at Culloden Muir, who died in 1854, re property in Queen Street, Inverness, on 1 October 1891. [NRS.S/H]

ANDERSON, WILLIAM, born 1808, son of William Anderson, died in Troy, USA, on 9 June 1842. [Westerkirk gravestone, Dumfriesshire]

ANDERSON, WILLIAM, in Philadelphia, Pennsylvania, ultimus haeres, 30 March 1882. [NRS.PS3.17y.70]

ANDERSON, WILLIAM, second son of James Anderson in Banchory-Ternan, Kincardineshire, died at Las Vegas, Nevada, on 1 January 1898. [AJ]

ANDREWS, THOMAS F., from America, graduated MD from Edinburgh University in 1819. [EMG]

ANDREWS, ROBERT, born 1858, son of William Andrews [1819-1914] and his wife Mary Milroy [1828-1908], died in Winnipeg, Manitoba, on 27 October 1882. [Colmonell gravestone, Ayrshire]

ANNAN, SAMUEL, from America, graduated MD from Edinburgh University in 1819. [EMG]

ANNAND, BANNERMAN, born 1841, from Kemnay, Aberdeenshire, died in Fredericton, New Brunswick, on 26 April 1874. [AJ]

ANNAND, Mrs MARY, wife of John Annand a carpenter from Aberdeen, died in Toronto, Ontario, on 28 March 1873. [AJ]

ANNAND, WILLIAM, born in Aberdeen, a printer who died in Nova Scotia in 1833. [AJ]

ARCHER, ..., son of Mrs Archer, was born at Olds, Canada, on 11 January 1898.[S.17037]

ARCHIBALD, ROBERT, minister of St Andrew's, Chatham, New Brunswick, from 1834 until he returned to Scotland in 1844. [F.7.608]

ARMIT, ANDREW, a minister in Pictou, Nova Scotia, from 1893 until 1896. [F.7.613]

ARMSTRONG, Major WILLIAM, in New York, a letter to Charles Williamson dated 1803. [NRS.GD364.1.1168]

ARTHUR, WILLIAM, in Brooklyn, New York, an inventory, 1876. [NRS.SC70.179.850]

BAILLIE, CHARLES, in Dalhousie, New Brunswick, a letter, 1829. [NLS.ms3908.1]

BAIN, JAMES, born in Madderty, Perthshire, in 1802, son of Peter Bain an artificer, educated at Glasgow University, emigrated to Canada in 1854, a minister in Ontario from1854 to 1874, died in Markham, Ontario, on 9 December 1885. [F.7.625]

BAIN, JOHN IRELAND TUCKER, in Brooklyn, New York, heir to his grandmother Elizabeth McEwan, wife of John Bain in Edinburgh, who died on 29 January 1855, 6 August 1889. [NRS.S/H]

BAIRD, GEORGE ALEXANDER, born 1862, son of George Baird in Strichen, Aberdeenshire, died in New Orleans, Louisiana, on 18 March 1893. [AJ]

BAIRD, JANET, in Tarbolton, Canada, in 1846. [NRS.SCPerth.46.51]

BAIRD, or FRASER, MARGARET JANE, wife of William J. Baird in Hopewell, New York was served heir to her uncle Donald Fraser in Porterfield, Inverness, who died on 20 March 1869. [NRS.S/H]

BAIRD, ROBERT MACGREGOR, eldest son of Charles R. Bard in Glasgow, died near Golden City in British Columbia, in November 1884. [S.12971]

BALFOUR, THOMAS, in Halsey, Linn County, Oregon, a sasine dated 19 May 1892. [NRS.RS.Kirkcaldy.27.43]

BALLINGALL, or HUTTON, MARGARET, in Halifax, Nova Scotia, heir to her brother James Ballingall in Kirkness House, Kinross, who died on 27 March 1885, 16 March 1887. [NRS.S/H]

BALLINGALL, ROBERT, from Balmacolm, Kettle, Fife, in 1782, died in Ayr, Ontario, on 21 November 1872; his wife Margaret Barclay, born 14 November 1788, daughter of Reverend Peter Barclay in Kettle, died in Duddington, Ontario, on 9 August 1856. [FH]

BAMBERRY, ROBERT, in Pondville, USA, heir to his mother Maria Mercer Mackie, wife of Robert Bamberry in Edinburgh, who died on 4 October 1899, 13 January 1900. [NRS.S/H]

BANNERMAN, Sir ALEXANDER, Governor of Newfoundland, a letter dated 1839. [NLS.ms221/125-8]

BANNERMAN, Lieutenant Colonel JOHN ALEXANDER, Governor of Prince of Wales Island around 1825. [NRS.CS96.1861]

BARCLAY, DAVID LYONS, son of George Barclay, settled on Fairview Farm, Pickering, Ontario, by 1840. [LAC.MG25.G272]

BARCLAY, GEORGE, in Brooklyn, USA, heir to his mother Margaret Graham, wife of William Barclay a sculptor in Millport, who died on 14 May 1872, re property in Millport, Bute, 13 December 1900. [NRS.S/H]

BARCLAY, JAMES, born 1790 in Montrose, Angus, died in Bermuda on 11 March 1831. [St Peter and St George gravestone, Bermuda]

BARCLAY, JAMES ALEXANDER, born 1870, only son of James Barclay in Gordon Place, Dyce, died at 53 Bates Street, Rochester, New York, on 24 February 1890. [AJ]

BARCLAY, PETER, in Hazlegreen, Wisconsin, an inventory, 1876. [NRS.SC70.178.840]

BARKER, JACOB W., from America, graduated CM from Glasgow University in 1827, possibly Wharton Barker, son of Jacob Barker a financier. [RGG]

BARR, or MCCULLOCH, CHRISTIE, in Hartford, Connecticut, a deed of factory and commission with Alexander Barr, dated 1882. [NRS.RD.1862.145.158]

BARRON, DAVID MYLNE, born 1852, late of Drumore, Pitcaple, died in Newhaven, Connecticut, on 20 August 1887. [AJ]

BARRY, CHALES HENDERSON, in New York in 1845. [NRS.SCPerth.45.60]

BART, ABRAM, in Pennsylvania, a letter to Margaret Colquhoun in Paisley, Renfrewshire, dated 6 June 1834. [NRS.GD1.814.6.2]

BAXTER, JEMIMA NICOLINA, born 10 July 1814, daughter of Reverend David Baxter and his wife Ann Campbell, married Reverend William King in Nelson, Ontario, died in 1887. [F.2.183]

BAYARD, SAMUEL, from Nova Scotia, graduated MD from Edinburgh University in 1826. [EMG]

BAYLEY, THOMAS ELDER, a merchant in Franklin, USA, an inventor in 1875. [NRS.SC70.174.18]

BEATTIE, JOHN, born 1809, youngest son of Dr Beattie in Insch, Aberdeenshire, died in Aurora, Wisconsin Territory in 1839. [AJ]

BEATTY, JOHN ROBERT, in Claytonville, Illinois, heir to his mother Helen Roy McLeran or Beatty in Salem, Ohio, who died on 10 June 1886, re property in Glasgow, 24 May 1887. [NRS.S/H]

BECK, WILLIAM J., in Morrisania, USA, an inventory dated 1878. [NRS.SC70.190.918]

BECKBLACK, BELLA, born 1880, youngest daughter of Alexander Beckblack, a mason from New Deer, Aberdeenshire, died in Hallowell, Maine, on 1 March 1882. [AJ]

BEGG, WILLIAM, born 1796 in Scotland, a schoolmaster in Goderich, Canada, died in Clinton, Canada, in 1864. [GM.ns2/17.256]

BEGG, WILLIAM PROUDFOOT, minister of Woodstock, New Brunswick, in 1872. [F.7.608]

BELL, ALEXANDER, in Canada, a deed of factory and commission, dated 11 December 1862. [NRS.RD1172.260]

BELL, JAMES, born 1838 in Castle Douglas, Dumfries-shire, died in New Orleans, Louisiana, in 1860. [Kelton gravestone]

BELL, PATRICK, journal of a journey through the northeastern USA and Canada between 1833 and 1837. [AUL.2137-8] [NRS.NRAS.O513]

BELL, WALTER, born 1836 in Castle Douglas, Dumfries-shire, died in New York in 1864. [Kelton gravestone]

BERFORD, H. R. F., in Canada, a deed dated 30 June 1828. [NRS.RD421.205]

BERRY, ROBERT, formerly a barrister in Hamilton, Upper Canada, was granted the lands of Torphin, Aberdeenshire, on 30 July 1856. [RGS.257.20.78]

BERTRAM, or MITCHELL, MARGARET, wife of Peter Bertram, a hardware merchant in Hamilton, Ontario, was served heir to her father Adam Mitchell, a master miller in Edinburgh, who died on 30 April 1879. [NRS.S/H]

BERWICK, DAVID, born 1841, died in Oakland, California, on 19 July 1878. [St Andrews Cathedral gravestone, Fife]

BEST, MARY AMELIA, wife of William Leslie Chalmers, died in San Francisco, California, on 15 February 1881. [AJ]

BETHUNE, ALEXANDER NEIL, Rector of Coburg, Canada, graduated DD at King's College, Aberdeen, on 6 March 1847. [KCA]

BEVERIDGE, ROBERT, an assayer from Crossgates, Fife, died in Jerome, Arizona, aged 39. [PJ]

BIRD, ROBERT, MD, in Cobham, Virginia, a deed in 1881. [NRS.RD.1689.237.212]

BIRKMYRE, JOHN, minister of St Paul's, Fredericton, New Brunswick, from 1832 until 1841 when he returned to Scotland. [F.7.608]

BISSET, HENRY, in Palmyra, Wisconsin, heir to his aunt Grace Bisset, a millworker in Dunfermline, Fife, who died in July 1882, 19 December 1887. [NRS.S/H]

BISSET, JAMES D., born 1868, eldest son of John Bisset in Woodside, Aberdeenshire, died in Albion, New York, in 1890. [AJ]

BLACK, JAMES, in Ottawa, Kansas, was served heir to his brother William Dalziel Black in Salsburgh, Shotts, Lanarkshire, who died on 11 September 1895. [NRS.S/H]

BLACK, JOHN, a farmer in Helloville, Mississippi, discharged the executors of Jane Black, a deed dated 1882. [NRS.RD.1880.42.295]

BLACK, THOMAS, from Aberdour, Fife, died in Cleveland, Ohio, on 3 April 1882. [Dunfermline Journal]

BLACKWOOD, THOMAS, in Montreal, letters, dated 1802, also 1828-1830. [NLS.ms3437/14, 73, 106, 188-97; ms3438/5, 13]

BOAG, Captain, a merchant in Greenock trading with Virginia and Baltimore in Maryland on the Peggy, a brigantine, in 1802. [NRS.CS229.Misc.16/6]

BONNER, JOSEPH, born 1851, late of St Nicholas Street, Aberdeen, died at 21 Garfield Street, Quincy, Massachusetts, in 1893. [AJ]

BONNYMAN, JOHN, born 1838, a granite dealer, died in Barre, Vermont, late of Aberdeen, died on 2 January 1898. [AJ]

BOOTH, JOHN, eldest son of William Booth in Hay Cottage, New Bridge of Don, Aberdeenshire, died at 60 Bank Street, New York, on 24 September 1895. [AJ]

BOOTH, JOHN SIM, an engineer in Kingston, Michigan, was served heir to his mother Jean Park, wife of John Booth a mason in Aberdeen, who died on 11 December 1896. [NRS.S/H]

BOWMAN, JAMES, of Fosterdale, America, Power of Attorney granted to James Bowman jr., dated 7 January 1863. [NRS.RD]

BOWRIN, PETER B., in Canada, a Deed of Factory and Commission in favour of William Whyte, dated 13 August 1853. [NRS.RD.1646.117]

BOYD, JAMES TOWER, son of George Boyd formerly a merchant in Ceylon, was educated at Marischal College in Aberdeen around 1847, later a banker in Brantford, Canada. [MCA]

BRERETON, R. M., in Forest Grove, Oregon, former factor of the Duke of Sutherland, a letter recommending emigration to Oregon, dated 1890, [NRS.NRAS.0852]

BROCKIE, WILLIAM, an insurance agent in Philadelphia, Pennsylvania, was served heir to the Trustees of John Manderson a druggist in Edinburgh on 8 June 1899. [NRS.S/H]

BRODIE, ALEXANDER OSWALD, born 1788, a merchant in New York, died in Edinburgh on 9 September 1856. [GM.ns2/1.526]

BRODIE, ANGUS, with a family of seven persons, from Loggantwine, Arran, bound for Canada, aboard the brigantine Caledonia in 1829, landed in Quebec on 25 June 1829. [TNA.CO384.22.3-5]

BRODIE, Mrs ELIZABETH, in New York, granted Duncan Cameron a deed of factory on 28 May 1832. [NRS.RD472.34.186]

BROOKS, ABRAHAM, born 1832, a joiner from Perth, an emigrant aboard the Annie Jane of Liverpool, master William Mason, bound from Liverpool to Quebec, was shipwrecked but survived near Vatersay in the Outer Hebrides on 28 September 1853. [WAJ]

BROOKS, JOHN, born 1836, a farm servant from Perth, an emigrant aboard the Annie Jane of Liverpool, master William Mason, bound from Liverpool to Quebec, was shipwrecked but survived near Vatersay in the Outer Hebrides on 28 September 1853. [WAJ]

BROWN, ANDREW, born in East Fife in 1789, emigrated to America, settled in Natchez, Mississippi, died there on 28 January 1871. [East Fife Record][Natchez Courier]

BROWN, ANNIE, second daughter of Hugh Reid in the Mains of Sauchen, Cluny, Aberdeenshire, wife of James Brown a stonecutter, died in Barre, Vermont, on 24 November 1894. [AJ]

BROWN, DAVID, fourth son of Archibald Brown in Inverdovat, Forgan Fife, died in Quebec on 29 December 1869. [FH]

BROWN, EDWARD, a millwright in Buffalo, New York, heir to his grandfather Edward Brown, a wright in Innerwick, East Lothian, who died on 6 November 1836, 17 October 1889. [NRS.S/H]

BROWN, GEORGE CAMPBELL, born 1889, only son of David and Jane Brown late of Aberdeen, died at 401, East 80th Street, New York, on 27 January 1891. [AJ]

BROWN, JAMES W., in North America, a discharge dated 27 February 1863. [NRS.RD1175.277]

BROWN, JAMES, in New York, a Deed of Factor and Commission, to William Kennedy, a Writer to the Signet, dated on 7 July 1863. [NRS.RD1183.592]

BROWN, JAMES, second son of the late Alexander Brown of the Kincardineshire Constabulary, died in Boston, Massachusetts, on 3 January 1893. [AJ]

BROWN, JOHN, born 1803, a farmer from Aberdeen, died in Maple Grove, Manitowoe, Wisconsin, on 20 February 1884. [AJ]

BROWN, JOSEPH, in Fort Worth, Texas, third son of William Brown a corn merchant in Newport, Fife, died in Brooklyn Avenue, Kansas City, on 26 October 1890. [FJ]

BROWN, MAGGIE, wife of William Brown, a stonecutter, eldest daughter of Hugh Reid in the Mains of Sauchen, Cluny, Aberdeenshire, died at Barre, Vermont, on 6 February 1894. [AJ]

BROWN, RACHEL, in Mearville, Pennsylvania, in 1877. [NRS.SC70.182.1018]

BRUCE, ARTHUR, born 1761, from Greenock, died in Geneva, USA, on 5 October 1843. [SG.1240]

BRUCE, HUGH, born 1872, youngest son of Alexander Bruce, mill manager of the Northern Cooperative Company, died in Durango, Colorado, in 1895. [AJ]

BRUCE, JOHN, born 1836, a stonecutter from Auchmill, Aberdeenshire, died at Barre, Vermont, in 1891. [AJ]

BRUCE, WALTER HAMILTON, in Montreal, Quebec, an inventory dated 1875. [NRS.SC70.175.204]

BRUCE, ..., son of the Countess of Elgin, was born at Spencer Wood, Upper Canada, on 26 April 1853. [GM.ns40.84]

BRUCE-GARDYNE, THOMAS W., of Middleton, Angus, formerly a Lieutenant of the 40th Regiment, married Annie Willard, daughter of Charles Willard in Kingston, Canada West, there on 6 April 1858. [GM.ns2/4.185]

BUCHANAN, WILLIAM BLACK, in Sanford, Florida, heir to his mother Janet Leidenroth, wife of Daniel Buchanan in

Tighnabruaich, Argyll, who died on 21 November 1891, re property there, 16 February 1900. [NRS.S/H]

BUCKLEY, JOHN, in Elora, Ontario, heir to his uncle John Buckley a gravedigger in Stonehouse, Lanarkshire, who died on 21 November 1890, 12 September 1891. [NRS.S/H]

BURLEIGH, Captain, master of the Washington of Portsmouth, New Hampshire, was wrecked off North Ronaldsay, Orkney, papers 1849. [NRS.NRAS.1222]

BURNESS, Mrs JOHN, born 1823, from Seagate in Montrose in Angus, and Aberdeen, died in Omaha, Nebraska, on 31 December 1888. [AJ]

BURNETT, CHARLES, born 1827, from Forfar in Angus, a seaman aboard the Annie Jane of Liverpool bound from Liverpool with emigrants bound for Quebec, was shipwrecked off Vatersey in the Outer Hebrides in 1853 but survived. [WAJ]

BURNETT, JAMES, born 1880, son of Hugh Burnett [1844-1928] and his wife Jessie Davidson [1850-1934], died 24 April 1912 in Montana, USA. [Banchory-Ternan gravestone, Aberdeenshire]

BURNET, JOHN, in Chicago, Illinois, heir to his cousin Betty Barnet, widow of James Rae a weaver in Forfar, Angus, who died on 14 March 1888, 29 October 1889. [NRS.S/H]

BURNETT, JOSEPH, born 28 February 1865 in St Nicholas, Aberdeen, son of John Burnett, graduated MA from Aberdeen University in 1887, a journalist on the staff of the Daily Record, Alleghany, Pennsylvania. [AUL]

BURNET, WILLIAM, from Aberdeen, a sailor in Philadelphia, Pennsylvania, brother and heir of Alexander Burnet a merchant in Aberdeen, 23 March 1793. [NRS.S/H]

BURNS, PETER, in Ontario, a letter dated 1871, to his cousin Robert Burns re family deaths in the Southern States. [NRS.NRAS.0091]

BURNS, ROBERT, born 13 February 1789 in Bo'ness, West Lothian, son of John Burns and his wife Grizel Ferrier, was educated at Edinburgh University, minister of Knox Church in Toronto from 1845 to 1856, a Professor in Knox College there from 1856 until 1864, died there on 19 August 1869. [F.3.176]

BURNS, ROBERT FERRIER, son of the above, born 23 December 1826, minister in Kingston, Canada, from 1847 until 1855, at St Catherine's, Canada, from 1855 to 1867, in Chicago, Illinois, from 1867 to 1870, in Montreal, Quebec from 1870 to 1875, in Halifax, Nova Scotia, in 1875, died in Broughty Ferry, Dundee, on 5 April 1896. [F]

BURTON, JOHN, from America, graduated MD from Edinburgh University in 1826. [EMG]

CADENHEAD, ALEXANDER S., son of Alexander Cadenhead an advocate in Aberdeen, was educated at Marischal College in Aberdeen around 1840, emigrated to Canada. [MCA]

CAIRNCROSS, JOHN, son of James Cairncross in Toronto, Ontario, was educated at Marichal College in Aberdeen around 1845, later was a clothier in Cullen, Banffshire. [MCA]

CALDER, DAVID, a rope-maker from Edinburgh, an emigrant aboard the Annie Jane of Liverpool, master William Mason, bound from Liverpool to Quebec, was shipwrecked but survived near Vatersay in the Outer Hebrides on 28 September 1853. [WAJ]

CAMERON, ALLAN, from Owen Sound, Ontario, graduated MD from Glasgow University in 1853. [RGG]

CAMERON, DONALD, born 1791, with his children Catherine born 1819, Christy born 1822, John born 1827, Ann born 1829, Ewen born 1836, also Ann McLellan born 1844, and James McLellan, from North Uist, emigrated via Greenock aboard the Cashmere of Glasgow bound for Quebec in 1849. [NRS.GD2214011.53]

CAMERON, DUGALD, a merchant grocer in Greenock, trading with Montreal and Demerara from 1825 until 1831. [NRS.CS96.866]

CAMERON, JOHN, at La Chene, Montreal, Quebec, in 1805. [NRS.GD202.70.12]

CAMPBELL, ARCHIBALD H., in Montreal, Quebec, a marriage contract with Louisa Fisher, dated 2 April 1856. [NRS.RD.1847.622.48]

CAMPBELL, COLIN, formerly an Ensign of the Orange Rangers a letter from Colonel John Campbell of the 74th Regiment, dated 8 March 1784. [NRS.GD170.3170]

CAMPBELL, or ESSON, in Belleville, Ontario a deed of factory with Helen Campbell, dated 1882. [NRS.1861.487.155]

CAMPBELL, GEORGE, a banker in Piper City, Illinois, a deed in 1882. [NRS.RD1883.178.322],

CAMPBELL, JANE ATHOL GORDON, daughter of John Campbell in Argyll, and widow of Major Thomas Fortye of the 8th Regiment, died in Toronto, Ontario, on 22 March 1864. [GM.ns2/16.805]

CAMPBELL, JOHN, in North America, power of attorney to William B. Penman, dated 28 August 1862. [NRS.RD1194.378]

CAMPBELL, LOUISA, of Melford, Argyll, journal of a tour of the USA and Canada in 1850. [NRS.NRAS.0853]

CAMPBELL, MALCOLM, in Edmonton, Alberta, heir to his grandmother Jane MacConachie Stuart or Campbell in Aberdeen, who died on 8 January 1889, 16 January 1900. [NRS.S/H]

CAMPBELL, Mrs MARGARET, born in Scotland in 1782, died in Fayetteville District, North Carolina, of consumption in December 1849. [FMS/NC]

CAMPBELL, RACHEL, spouse of Adam Ferre, late of Glasgow, now of Montreal, Quebec, a deed in 1837. [NRS.GD64.1.320]

CAMPBELL, Captain ROBERT, born 1776 in Greenock, died in Georgia in 1818. [Colonial Museum and Savanna Advertiser, 1. April 1818]

CAMPBELL, ROBERT, in Sanilac or Twining, Arenac County, Michigan, letters, 1871-1885. [GCA.TD902/1-3]CAMPBELL, WILLIAM PATRICK, born 10 January 1819, son of William Campbell a merchant in USA, educated at Edinburgh Academy from 1828 to 1829. [EAR]

CAMPBELL, WILLIAM, from Skye, Inverness-shire, emigrated via Greenock aboard the Royal Adelaide bound for St John, New Brunswick, later to Fredericton, petitioned the New Brunswick House of Assembly in 1838. [PANB.RS24/4/77]

CAMPBELL, PETER, in St Louis, Missouri, an inventory dated 1878. [NRS.SC70.187.779]

CAMPBELL, ROBERT, from Glasgow, settled in Arenac County, Michigan, by 1871, letters from 1871 until 1885. [GCA.GB243.TD902]

CAMPBELL, THOMAS D., in Canada, a deed in favour of P. W. Campbell, dated 1 December 1857. [NRS.RD1052.623]

CAMPBELL, WILLIAM, born 1877, a stonecutter from Aberdeen, died in Boston, Massachusetts, on 30 April 1900. [AJ]

CANTLEY, ISABELLA, youngest daughter of John Cantley a farmer in Auquharney, Cruden, Aberdeenshire, died at Lompoc, Santa Barbara, California, on 22 January 1893. [AJ]

CARDEAN, DAVID, in Fredericksburg, Maryland, discharged his trustees in 1882. [NRS.RD1871.82.223]
CARDEAN, DAVID, in Fredericksburg, Maryland, discharged his trustees in 1882 [NRS.RD1871/82.223]

CARDNO, JOHN, a, JOHN, a ships carpenter in New Orleans, Louisiana, was served heir to his father James Cardno, a carter in Firth Street, Fraserburgh, Aberdeenshire, who died on 6 April 1875. [NRS.S/H]

CARLYLE, JOHN, a farmer in Delhi, Ontario, a letter, 1878. [NLS.ms1775G/198]

CARNEGIE, ANDREW, born 1835 in Dunfermline, Fife, emigrated to America in 1848, a Trust Deed dated December 1913. [NRS.RD15.1.4]

CARPENTER, SAMUEL, from America, a student at Marischal College in Aberdeen in 1759. [MCA]

CARR, or GRAHAM, MARTHA, wife of Patrick Graham in Palatka, Florida, to her brother Bryan or Bernard Carr in Lennoxtown, who died on 29 March 1886, re property in Kilsyth, Stirlingshire, 4 February 1887. [NRS.S/H]

CARSWELL, THOMAS W. B., in Guelph, Canada, an inventory, dated 1878. [NRS.SC70.187.688]

CARTER, MARGARET, born 1820, youngest daughter of David Carter in Aberdeen, died in Chicago, Illinois, in 1896. [AJ]

CASSIDY, MARY, born 1833, a mill worker from Kilmarnock, Ayrshire, with her son Daniel Cassidy, born 1853, emigrants aboard the Annie Jane of Liverpool, master William Mason, bound from Liverpool to Quebec, was shipwrecked and drowned near , Vatersay in the Outer Hebrides on 28 September 1853. [WAJ]

CHALMERS, Mr formerly clerk of Mr Morrison in Leith, now in St Augustine, East Florida proposed as agent there f Sir Archibald Grant in 1773. [?] [NRS.GD1.32.38]

CHALMERS, JOHN, born 1841, died in New York on 28 April 1850. [St Andrews Cathedral gravestone, Fife]

CHALMERS, JOHN, of 2028 Morgan Street, St Louis, Missouri, a deed of attorney in favour of James Scott, clothier in Freuchie, Fife, dated 26 April 1883. [NRS.B9.8.1/283-286]

CHALMERS, JOHN, in Scranton, Kansas, heir to his mother Jane Sneddon, widow of John Chalmers a miner in Slamannan, Falkirk, who died in September 1884, on 11 April 1887. [NRS.S/H]

CHISHOLM, WILLIAM, with Magdalen and Isabella, from Linn of Gorthleck, Inverness-shire, emigrants aboard the <u>Annie Jane of Liverpool</u>, master William Mason, bound from Liverpool to Quebec, were shipwrecked and drowned near Vatersay in the Outer Hebrides on 28 September 1853. [WAJ]

CHRISTIE, BETSY, wife of Henry Christie and daughter of George Christie in the Mains of Lindores, Fife, died in Chelsea, Massachusetts, on 14 February 1859. [Fife Herald]

CHRISTIE, DONALD, settled in Reach, Ontario, by 1848, a petitioner. [NRS.GD112.61.5]

CHRISTIE, DUNCAN, settled in Reach, Ontario, by 1848, a petitioner. [NRS.GD112.61.5]

CHRISTIE, JAMES, from Kildrummy in Aberdeenshire, was educated at Marischal College in Aberdeen around 1846, later a missionary in Constantinople in Canada. [MCA]

CHRISTIE, JOHN, settled in Reach, Ontario, by 1848, a petitioner. [NRS.GD112.61.5]

CHRISTIE, or BLANEY, MARIANNE, in Port Haney, British Columbia, heir to her father David Christie a mason in Linlithgow, West Lothian, who died on 11 October 1873, re property in High Street, Linlithgow, on 30 March 1891. [NRS.S/H]

CHRISTIE, PETER, settled in Reach, Ontario, by 1848, a petitioner. [NRS.GD112.61.5]

CHRISTIE, WILLIAM, born 1823, eldest son of John Christie of the Royal Hotel, St Andrews, in Fife, died in Minnesota Territory, on 8 May 1852. [FJ]

CIRSOVIUS, Mrs H. and spouse, in New York, a deed in favour of Cowan and Pearson, on 28 May 1831. [NRS.RD438.337]

CLARK, ALEXANDER, in New Jersey, an inventory dated 1877. [NRS.SC70.184.1147]

CLARK, Mrs JANET HUTTON or, in Ontario, an inventory, dated 1874. [NRS.SC70.166.1040]18

CLARK, JOHN, with his wife Mary Grant, and their eight children, from Tomfad, Fhearnasdail, Glen Feshie, Inverness-shire, emigrated in 1833 to Puslinch, Upper Canada,

CLARK, WILLIAM, with his wife and nine children, Fhearnasdail, Glen Feshie, Inverness-shire, emigrated in 1833 to Puslinch, Upper Canada, [HS.16.4.17]

CLARK, WILLIAM, in Youngston, Ohio, an inventory dated 1877. [NRS.SC70.184.730]

CLEMENT, or SHIELLS, JACOBINA CATHERINE, in Milwaukee, Wisconsin, was served heir to Mary Swan and later to Janet Swan in Dollar, Clackmannanshire, who died on 28 April 1899 and 12 June 1888 respectively. [NRS.S/H]

CLOUSTON, EDWARD, late in Hudson Bay Company Service, 1803. [OA]

CLOW, ROBERT, in Oregon Precinct, Illinois, an inventory dated 1874. [NRS.SC70.167.645]

CLYDE, PETER, a lumber surveyor in Miramachi, New Brunswick, a letter, dated 28 June 1830. [NRS.GD1.620.84]

COCHRAN, JOHN, a cotton yard merchant in Glasgow, trading with Honduras, Mexico, and New York between 1828 and 1831. [NRS.CS96.690.1/2]

COCHRANE, Sir JOHN INGLIS, former Governor of Newfoundland, June 1837. [NRS.CS46.1837.6.63]

COCKBURN, or HADDOW, AGNES, in Tala, Illinois, heir to her father Thomas Cockburn a butcher in Litchfield, Illinois, who died 22 January 1868. [NRS.S/H]

COCKBURN, or ROBSON, ISABELLA, in Mattoon, Illinois, heir to her father Thomas Cockburn a butcher in Litchfield, Illinois, who died 22 January 1868. [NRS.S/H]

COCKBURN, or MCPHERSON, MARY, in Union, Franklin, heir to her father Thomas Cockburn a butcher in Litchfield, Illinois, who died 22 January 1868. [NRS.S/H]

COLLIER, JAMES CURRIE, in Dubuque, Iowa, was served heir to his father Robert Hutchison Collier, a company manager there, who died on 19 March 1896, re property in Ballplay Road, Moffat, Dumfries-shire. [NRS.S/H]

COLQUHOUN, JOHN, from Paisley, Renfrewshire, emigrated via Liverpool to America in November 1841, a letter to his mother, another from Rhode Island, in May 1842. [NRS.GD1.814.9.1-2]

COLQUHOUN and RITCHIE, merchants in Glasgow, trading with St John, Quebec, Wilmington, Virginia, Antigua, Jamaica, North Carolina and Grenada, between 1791 and 1809. [NRS.CS96.3994]

COLVILLE, THOMAS LOW, in Wilmington, USA, an inventory dated 1875. [NRS.SC70.171.347]

COMBE, ANDREW, born 1797, a physician in Edinburgh, emigrated via Liverpool aboard the Montezuma bound for New York in 1847, a letter re conditions aboard ship. [NRS.GD297.30]

CONSTABLE, WALTER, son of Thomas Constable, emigrated to America, a letter dated around 1872. [NRS.NRAS.0342.91]

COOK, ALEXANDER, from Cloined, Arran, settled in Inverness township, Megantic County, Quebec, in 1831. [TNA.CO384.28.24-26]

COOK, ARCHIBALD, from Mid Kiscadale, Arran, settled in Inverness township, Megantic County, Quebec, in 1831. [TNA.CO384.28.24-26]

COOK, HENRY WATSON, at Renton, Ontario, heir to his brother William Edgar Cook in Burntisland, Fife, who died on 9 March 1882, on 21 November 1889. [NRS.S/H]

COOK, JOHN, from Arran, emigrated via Lamlash aboard the brigantine Caledonia bound for Canada in 1829, landed in Quebec on 25 June 1829. [TNA.CO384.28.24/26]

CORBET, WILLIAM, a blacksmith from Glasgow, with his wife Catherine Reekie or Corbet, and daughter Helen Millar Corbet born 1844, also their son William Corbet aged 1846, emigrants aboard the Annie Jane of Liverpool, master William Mason, bound from Liverpool to Quebec, was shipwrecked and drowned near Vatersay in the Outer Hebrides on 28 September 1853. [WAJ]

COTTER, DANIEL, born in Glasgow, a glass stainer and designer, died in Florida, letters dated 1878. [UAL.GB231, ms2123]

CRAIG, CHARLES XAVIER, an artist and engraver in Hoboken, New Jersey, heir to his uncle John Craigje, a bank accountant in Dumfries, who died on 30 January 1848, re property in Castle Douglas, Kirkcudbrightshire, on 10 January 1887. [NRS.S/H]

CRAN, WILLIAM, born 1846, son of Peter Cran auctioneer in Ballater, Aberdeenshire, died in Toronto, on 8 November 1877, [Glen Muick gravestone]; an inventory dated 1878. [NRS.SC70.187.1095]

CRAWFORD, DANIEL, from Arran, with a family of nine, settled in Inverness, Lower Canada, in 1831. [TNA.CO384.28.24/26]

CRAWFORD, JOHN, merchant in Port Glasgow, trading with Newfoundland from 1816 until 1817. [NRS.CS96.335]

CRAWFORD, WILLIAM, with a family of two persons, from Corrie, Arran, bound for Canada, 1829. [TNA.CO384.22.3-5]

CRICHTON, Mrs HELEN, from Dundee, Angus, wife of James Crichton, a merchant in Pictou, Nova Scotia, a letter to her uncle Aaron Lithgow a merchant in Dundee, dated 18 December 1837. [NLS.ms2543.fos 37-38]

CRIGHTON, Dr JOHN P., in East Florida, a Deed of Factory and Commission dated 18 July 1855. [NRS.RD.1178.453]

CROLL, ANDREW, born 1821, son of Charles Croll and his wife Janet Mitchell, died in Quebec on 18 June 1848. [St Andrews Cathedral gravestone, Fife]

CROSS, or RATTRAY, CHRISTINA in Yorkhill, Ontario, a Deed of Attorney in favour of John Watson dated 1882. [NRS.RD1868.644.209]

CRUICKSHANK, or PETRIE, SUSANNA, in Lebanon, Stephen's City, Virginia, heir to her sister Janet Mackintosh Cruickshank of Broomhill, Lochmaben, Dumfries-shire, who died on 24 July 1900, [NRS.S/H]

CUMMING, ALEXANDER BEATTIE, in De Witt, Iowa, heir to his brother Robert Cumming, a retired bookseller in Doune, Stirlingshire, who died 8 February 1890. [NRS.S/H]

CUMMING, JACOBINA, born 1833, daughter of John Cumming [1800-1879], and his wife Elizabeth Bell, [1807-1868], wife of James Russell, died in Canada on 28 January 1868. [Maybole gravestone, Ayrshire]

CUMMING, JANET BALLOCH or, in Brant, Ontario, an inventory dated 1875. [NRS.SC70.175.921]

CUMMING, JOHN, from Largymeanoch, Arran, settled in Inverness township, Megantic County, Quebec, in 1831. [TNA.CO384.28.24-26]

CUNNINGHAM, ADAM, born in Kirkcaldy, Fife, in 1820, died in Chicago, Illinois, on 13 November 1903. [FFP]

CUTHBERT, Miss JANET, at Grand Rapids, Michigan, an inventory dated 1874. [NRS.SC70.169.293]

DAGGETT, PHILADER, in New York, an inventory dated 1875. [NRS.SC70.175.685]

DALGLEISH, THOMAS, a tinsmith in Canada, an inventory dated 1876. [NRS.SC70.180.374]

DALLAS, JAMES, in Ontario, an inventory dated 1872. [NRS.SC70.160.450]

DALLAS, PETER, in Alabama, an inventory dated 1877. [NRS.SC70.182.109]

DALYELL, JOHN JAMES, a letter book from 1868 to 1872, refers to members of the Rock Ferry Scottish Brigade in America. [NRS.NRAS.01220.42]

DALY, or CARR, ROSE ANN, wife of James Daly in Streator, Illinois, heir to her brother Bryan or Bernard Carr in Lennoxtown, who died on 29 March 1886, re property in Kilsyth, Stirlingshire, 4 February 1887. [NRS.S/H]

DARLING, GEORGINA CARSTAIRS, daughter of William Darling, a writer [lawyer] in Dunfermline, Fife, died on Catalina Island, California, on 29 July 1897. [DJ]

DARLING, WILLIAM, in Canada, an inventory dated 1871. [NRS.SC70.153.442]

DAVIDSON, ANNIE, in Appleton City, Missouri, heir to her grandfather John Davidson a merchant in Aberdeen, who died on 2 December 1853. [NRS.S/H]

DAVIDSON, CHARLES, born 1848, son of James Davidson in Ladiesford, Aberdeenshire, and his wife Elizabeth Rankin, died in Rockland, Maine, on 28 September 1872. [Aberdour gravestone]

DAVIDSON, or PRESTON, Mrs EUPHEMIA, in Albany City, USA, an inventory dated 1874. [NRS.SC70.169.971]

DAVIDSON, GEORGE, in Waterloo, Ontario, heir to John Paul a farmer in Over Kirkton of Dyce, Aberdeenshire, re a share of subjects in Longacre, Aberdeen. [NRS.S/H]

DAVIDSON, NANCY WOODBURN, in Appleton City, Missouri, heir to her grandfather John Davidson a merchant in Aberdeen, who died on 2 December 1853. [NRS.S/H]

DAVIES, THOMAS, in Cleveland, Ohio, heir to his mother Janet Stewart, wife of Thomas Davies a brickmaker in Alloa, Clackmannanshire, who died on 20 June 1860, on 21 February 1889. [NRS.S/H]

DEUCHAR, ALLAN, son of William Deuchar a farmer in America, was educated at Marichal College in Aberdeen around 1841. [MCA]

DIAS or STEWART, MARGARET, in Brooklyn, America, heir to her mother Jean Swan, who died on 8 July 1883, wife of Thomas Stewart in Glasgow. [NRS.S/H]

DICK, SAMUEL RICHARD FINLAYSON, a lapidary in Montreal, Quebec, ultimus haeres, 31 October 1874. [NRS.PS3.17.19]

DICKIE, GEORGE, son of William Dickie in New Buildings, Springfield, Fife, late in Montrose, Angus, died in New Brunswick on 29 April 1900. [PJ]

DICKSON, ALEXANDER GILLESPIE, in Toronto, Ontario, heir to his father John Dickson a tailor and clothier in Amisfield, Tinwald, Dumfries-shire, who died on 31 March 1883. [NRS.S/H]

DICKSON, or BLACK, JESSIE, wife of William Black in Montreal, Quebec, heir to her brother George Dickson a blacksmith in Dalbeattie, Dumfries-shire, who died on 23 November 1890, 25 June 1891. [NRS.S/H]

DODDS, JAMES H., a gold prospector in Dawson City, Alaska, a letter dated 18 March 1898. [NLS.Acc.6665]

DONALD, ALEXANDER G., in King's Park, Nova Scotia, a deed in 1882. [NRS.RD.1852.324.316]

DOUGAL, JOHN, railway manager in Lima, Ohio, heir to his father John Dougal, a contractor in Falkirk, Stirlingshire, who died on 5 August 1899, re property there, 21 July 1900. [NRS.S/H]

DOUGLAS, ALEXANDER, from Watten, Caithness, settled in Kingston, Quebec, by 1841. [JGJ,19.2.1841]

DOUGLAS, CHARLES IRVINE, son of Lord William Douglas, married Margaret Elizabeth Holmstead, daughter of Arthur Holmes in Toronto, Ontario, there on 4 March 1862. [GM.ns2/17.840]

DOW, ALEXANDER DRYSDALE, in Honolulu, Hawaii, an inventory dated 1876. [NRS.SC70.178.676]

DREW, JAMES, in Bingham County, Idaho, heir to his cousin James Drew, a labourer in Stewarton, Ayrshire, who died on 1 June 1887, [NRS.S/H]

DRYBURGH, Reverend ANDREW, in Elmira, Canada, an inventory dated 1878. [NRS.SC70.188.972]

DRYSDALE, ROBERT HUNTER, from Dunfermline, a Captain of the 3rd Regiment of the Confederate Army, died in North Carolina, on 16 January 1863. [FH]

DUFF, JAMES, an Ensign of the 74th Regiment, stationed at Quebec, Montreal, and La Prairie, sixteen letters dated between 1841 and 1845. [Royal Highland Fusiliers Museum]

DUFF, ROBERT POPE ROSS, born 20 July 1828 son of Hugh Duff, a farmer, and his wife Johanna Ross, in Edderton, Ross-shire, a merchant, who died in San Francisco, California, on 9 February 1903. [San Francisco Call] [Nigg gravestone]

DUNCAN, CHARLES, born 1831, son of Henry Duncan of Brighton Tile and Brick Works in Cupar, Fife settled in Brantford, Ontario, married Jeannie Bell in Sheridan, New Brunswick, in 1858, died in Brantford on 7 October 1907. [FH]

DUNCAN, Mrs ISABEL, wife of William Duncan master of the Scotia of Banff, letters from American and West Indian ports dated from 1884 to 1886. [NRS.NRAS.0919]

DUNCANSON, ALEXANDER, son of Alexander Duncanson, a baker in Glasgow, and his wife Jean Cumming, died in Charleston, South Carolina, on 14 September 1838. [Ramshorn gravestone, Glasgow]

DUNLOP, ALEXANDER, in Montreal, Quebec, a letter dated 1827. [NLS.5308/482]

DUNLOP, COLIN MCKENZIE, in Virginia, an inventory dated 1876. [NRS.SC70.176.756]

DUNLOP, JAMES, in Petersburg, Virginia, a deed dated 19 April 1801. [NRS.RD402.6288]

DUNLOP, JOHN, letters from missionaries in America, between 1855 and 1860. [NRS.NRAS.1239]DUTHIE, DAVID, in Iowa, heir to his brother Joseph Duthie, a farmer in Hillhead of Heatherwick, Angus, who died on 25 July 1899, re property at Rennyfield, Montrose, Angus, dated 11 January 1900. [NRS.S/H]

ERSKINE, WILLIAM, in Canada, a Power of Attorney. [NRS.RD1194.108]

EVE, FRANCIS AUGUSTUS, in Bermuda, graduated MD from Edinburgh University in 1825. [EMG]

FAIR, JOHN, jr., a notary in Montreal, Quebec, heir to his mother Catherine Clark Rowat, wife of John Fair in Canada, who died on 24 February 1882, re property in Hamilton, Lanarkshire. 8 June 1887. [NRS.S/H]

FAIRBAIRN, EDWARD, in Buffalo, New York, heir to his mother Catherine Aitchison Bruce, wife of James Fairbairn in Hawick, Roxburghshire, who died on 14 October 1869, re property in Raeburn Place, Edinburgh, on 19 October 1891. [NRS.S/H]

FAIRLEY, JAMES, in Thornton, Providence, Rhode Island, was served heir to his father Hugh Fairley, a labourer in Bathgate, West Lothian, who died on 23 June 1897. [NRS.S/H]

FAIRLIE, WILLIAM, born 1860, son of James Fairlie and his wife Agnes Smith, died in Langoon, North Dakota, in 1892. [Monikie gravestone, Angus]

FALCONER JAMES, born 1808, a minister of the Church of Scotland, later of the Free Church, emigrated to Canada in 1851, possibly died there in 1856. [F.111.178]

FENDER, DAVID, a carpenter in La Grange, Ohio, heir to his uncle John Fender a farmer at the Backmuir of Liff, Angus, who died on 18 January 1890, re the lands of Kirkton of Liff, 12 June 1891. [NRS.S/H]

FERGUSON*, ADAM JOHNSTON, born 1816, son of advocate Adam Fergusson of Woodhill, Canada, was educated at Edinburgh Academy from 1824 to 1830. [*later Ferguson-Blair] [EAR]

FERGUSON, ALEXANDER, born 1842 in America, son of the late John Ferguson, died at Scouringburn, Dundee, on 1 November 1854. [St Peter's burial register, Dundee] FERGUSON, CHRISTY, born 1799, with Donald Mathieson born 1828, John Mathieson born 1831, from North Uist, Outer Hebrides, bound via Greenock aboard the Waterhen of London to Quebec in 1849. [NRS.GD221.4435]

FERGUSON, DANIEL, son of Robert Ferguson a merchant in Ristaguchi, New Brunswick, was educated at Marichal College in Aberdeen in 1842. [MCA]

FERGUSON, DAVID, born 1817, son of advocate Adam Ferguson of Woodhill, Canada, was educated at Edinburgh Academy from 1825 to 1830. [EAR]

FERGUSON, JAMES SCOTT, born 1820, son of advocate Adam Ferguson of Woodhill, Canada, was educated at Edinburgh Academy from 1827 to 1832. [EAR]

FERGUSON, JOHN, from Skye, emigrated via Greenock, Renfrewshire, aboard the Royal Adelaide bound for St John, New Brunswick, later to Fredericton, N.B., petitioned the New Brunswick House of Assembly in 1838. [PANB.RS24/4/77]

FERGUSON, MARY, born 1829, from North Uist, Outer Hebrides, Hebrides, emigrated via Greenock aboard the Cashmere of Glasgow bound for Quebec in 1849. [NRS.GD2214011.53]

FERGUSSON, ROBERT, in America, letters from 1856 to 1874. [DAC.GD226.GGD234]

FIFE, JAMES, son of Charles Fife in Kirkcaldy, died in Faribault, Rice County, Minnesota, on 29 February 1888. [FFP]

FINDLATER, GEORGE ROBERT, in New York, heir to his mother Margaret Finlayson or Findlater in Broughty Ferry, Angus, who died on 11 February 1890, re property in Arbroath, Angus. [NRS.S/H]

FINLAYSON, WILLIAM THOMAS, in Detroit, Michigan, an inventory, dated 1870. [NRS.SC70.197.144]

FISCHER, WILLIAM jr., a traveller in Toronto, Canada, heir to John Paul a farmer in Over Kirkton of Dyce, Aberdeenshire, re a share of subjects in Longacre, Aberdeen. [NRS.S/H]

FISHER, JOHN, in Chicago, Illinois, heir to his sister Jane Fisher in Edinburgh, she died on 11 May 1890, re property at 1 Windsor Street, Edinburgh. [NRS.S/H]

FLEMING, SANDFORD, born 1827, son of Andrew Fleming, a cabinetmaker in Kirkcaldy, Fife, and his wife Elizabeth Arnot, emigrated to Canada in 1845, a Civil Engineer, Chancellor of Queen's University, President of the Royal Society of Canada, graduated LL.D from St Andrews University in 1884, died 1915. [StAUR]

FLEMING, Reverend WILLIAM MARTIN, in Essex, Ontario, heir to his father William Fleming a mason in Strathaven, Lanarkshire, who died on 28 November 1889. [NRS.S/H]

FLETT, WILLIAM, in Hudson Bay Company Service, versus William Couston a tailor in Stromness, Orkney, in 1805. [OA]

FLOWERDEW, JAMES GRAY, merchant in Portland, USA, an inventory dated 1873. [NRS.SC70.165.423]

FORBES, ALEXANDER, a former Major of the 79th Highlanders, died in Kingston, Canada West, on 39 March 1851. [GM.ns36.216]

FORBES, FRANCIS, son of Sir C. Forbes, died in San Francisco, California, on 30 December 1849. [GM.ns33.559]

FORBES, ROBERT, born 1855, died in Leadmill, Colorado, on 12 December 1891. [St Andrews Cathedral gravestone, Fife]

FORSYTH, JOHN HERMAN, son of Alexander Forsyth a jeweller in Buenos Ayres, Argentina, graduated MA from Marischal College, in Aberdeen in 1841, enlisted in the United States Army. [MCA]

FORSYTH, ROBERT, in Brooklyn, New York, heir to his father Thomas Halliday Forsyth a coal merchant in Glasgow who died 24 January 1890, 12 September 1890. [NRS.S/H].

FORTUNE, JOHN, in Huntingdon, Quebec, heir to Ann Buchanan, widow of Andrew Adam, a weaver in Paisley, Renfrewshire, re property in Paisley, 2 April 1889. [NRS.S/H]

FRASER, DONALD, a joiner from Inverness, an emigrant aboard the <u>Annie Jane of Liverpool</u>, master William Mason, bound from Liverpool to Quebec, was shipwrecked but survived near Vatersay in the Outer Hebrides on 28 September 1853. [WAJ]

FRASER, JAMES, born 1800 in Fodderty, Ross-shire, was educated at the Universities of Aberdeen and Edinburgh, a schoolmaster in Lochinver, was ordained for missionary work in Cape Breton, Nova Scotia, was admitted to Boulardarie in 1837, died there on 8 April 1874. [F.7.607]

FRASER, JAMES N., born in Nova Scotia around 1829, a medical student in Edinburgh, 1851. [Census]

FRASER, JAMES WILLIAM, MA, was appointed as minister to the River Inhabitants in Cape Breton in 1866, went to Nova Scotia in 1870. [F.7.607]

FRASER, JANE HELEN, in New York, heir to her aunt Eliza Fraser in Peterhead, Aberdeenshire, who died on 13 July 1885, re property in Peterhead, 14 October 1887. [NRS.S/H]

FRASER, REBECCA HARRIOTT, daughter of John Fraser of Farraline, Inverness, an advocate, wife of Reverend John Gray, died in Kingston, Canada West, on 10 February 1851. [GM.ns.36.455]

FRASER, WILLIAM, a labourer from Inverness, an emigrant aboard the Annie Jane of Liverpool, master William Mason, bound from Liverpool to Quebec, was shipwrecked but survived near Vatersay in the Outer Hebrides on 28 September 1853. [WAJ]

FREELAND, Reverend WILLIAM, in Ottawa, an inventory dated 1873. [NRS.SC70.165.128]

FORBES, JOHN STUART, of the United States Army, an inventory dated 1877. [NRS.SC70.183.200]

FOTHERINGHAM, JAMES, in New Hampshire, an inventory dated 1877. [NRS.SC70.186.572]

FRASER, JOHN, in Nelson, British Columbia, was served heir to his mother Janet Buchanan Dow, wife of Thomas Fraser in Belfast, Ireland, who died on 9 October 1870. [NRS.S/H]

FULLARTON, ARCHIBALD, from Brodick, Arran, settled in Inverness township, Megantic County, Quebec, in 1831. [TNA.CO384.28.24-26]

FULLARTON, JAMES, with a family of seven persons, from Corrie, Arran, bound for Canada, 1829. [TNA.CO384.22.3-5]

FULTON, or MEIKLE, MARY STOREY, in Morrisburg, Ontario, heir to her aunt Isabella Duncan, widow of William Gemmell in Glasgow, who died on 5 January 1888, re property in Glasgow. [NRS.S/H]

FULTON, NORMAN, then in USA, letters from Dr Thomas Blackwood Murray, an electrical engineer, re design of a new car, dated 1899. [NRS.NRAS.0396]

GALLOWAY, ELIZABETH, born 1839, daughter of Edward Galloway, a fish-curer in Fraserburgh, Aberdeenshire, died in Canada on 13 February 1856. [Fraserburgh Kirkton gravestone]

GALLOWAY, MARY, born 1850, daughter of Edward Galloway a fish-curer in Fraserburgh, Aberdeenshire, died in Canada in 1864. [Fraserburgh Kirkton gravestone]

GALLOWAY, WILLIAM, born 1835, son of Edward Galloway a fish-curer in Fraserburgh, Aberdeenshire, died in Canada in December 1858. [Fraserburgh Kirkton gravestone]

GALLOWAY, family, in Savanna, Georgia, letters from 1854 until 1860. [NRS.NRAS.0744.4]

GALT, JOHN, Registrar of Huron County, at Goderich, Canada West, a letter, 1864. [NLS. Paton Collection, ms3217/100]

GARRIOCH, ALEXANDER, in California, granted Power of Attorney to John Murdoch, dated 2 February 1838. [NRS.RD1043.464]

GENTLE, ROBERT, formerly a farmer at Airdrie, Crail, Fife, died in South Carolina, on 6 July 1882. [EFR][DJ]

GEORGE, JAMES, Vice Principal of Kingston College, Upper Canada, a letter dated 1841. [NLS.ms3443/253]

GEORGE, JAMES, in Toronto, Ontario, an inventory dated 1879. [NRS.SC70.193.79]

GIBB, SARAH, in San Francisco, California, a Deed of Factory and Commission, dated 15 March 1856. [NRS.RD.1181.

GIBB, WILLIAM, a merchant in San Francisco, California, an inventory dated 1872. [NRS.SC70.198]

GIBSON, MARY ANN, born 1848 in Quebec, daughter of Andrew Gibson a private soldier of the 93rd Regiment, died in Dudhope Crescent, Dundee, was buried on 16 October 1854. [DCA]

GILLANDERS, FRANCIS, in Niantic, Connecticut, heir to his grandfather Francis Gillanders at Woodside, Aberdeen, who died on 31 May 1890, on 12 May 1891. [NRS.S/H]

GILLIS, JOHN, from Skye, Inverness-shire, emigrated via Greenock aboard the Royal Adelaide bound for St John, New Brunswick, later to Fredericton, N.B., petitioned the New Brunswick House of Assembly in 1838. [PANB.RS24/4/77]

GILLIS, SARAH, born 1760 in Scotland, died of old age in Fayetteville District, North Carolina, in January 1850. [FMS/NC]

GILMOUR, JAMES, in Ramsay, Lanark, Upper Canada, a Deed of Factory and Commission, dated 9 April 1833. [NRS.SC58.59.13.264]

GILMOUR, JOHN, in Ramsay, Lanark, Upper Canada, a Deed of Factory and Commission dated 9 April 1833. [NRS.SC58.59.13.264]

GILPIN, ALFRED, born in Nova Scotia around 1829, a medical student in Edinburgh, 1851. [Census]

GILSTRAP, or STEWART, ELLEN JANE, in Racine, Missouri, heir to her aunt Elizabeth Stewart in Castlepark, Auchterarder, Perthshire, who died on 23 April 1880, 28 January 1887. [NRS.S/H]; also, to her father Thomas Stewart at Fall Clove, New York, who died on 14 October 1855, on 5 March 1887. [NRS.S/H]

GOODWILLIE, ROBERT, from Aberdour, Fife, died in Montreal Quebec, on 18 October 1854. [Fife Herald]

GORDON, ALEXANDER, in Toronto, Ontario, an inventory dated 1871. [NRS.SC70.151.70]

GORDON, Sir ARTHUR, in Samoa, a letter stating that an expedition was about to sail from San Francisco, California, bound for Samoa, in 1878. [NRS.NRAS.0935]

GORDON, DANIEL, son of John Gordon a farmer at Blair Atholl in Perthshire, was educated at Marischal College in Aberdeen around 1842, later a Free Church minister in Montreal, Canada. [MCA]

GORDON, GEORGE H., was lost overboard from the Hera of Boston in 1870, statements. [NRS.NRAS.0055]

GORDON, HUGH DOUGLAS, born 1852 in Castle Douglas, died in Hapler, Kansas, in 1893. [Kelton gravestone, Kirkcudbrightshire]

GOULD, ROBERT, in North Adams, Massachusetts, heir to his father Robert Gould, a spirit merchant in Glasgow, who died in October 1886, re property in Glasgow, on 30 August 1889. [NRS.S/H]

GOWANS, THOMAS, a bricklayer in Cleveland, Ohio, heir to his father James Gowans, a grocer in Edinburgh, who died on 21 March 1876, re property in Edinburgh, on 1 February 1900. [NRS.S/H]

GRAFTON, GILBERT COLLINS, in Fargo, North Dakota, heir to his father Joseph Smith Grafton jr. an architect in Manchester England, who died on 9 July 1882, re property in Forfar, Angus, dated 8 March 1900. [NRS.S/H]

GRAHAME, JOHN, in Vaughan Township, Canada West, a letter dated 1849. [NLS.ms1775b/45]

GRANT, GEORGE MUNRO, born in Stellarton, Pictou, Nova Scotia, on 22 December 1835, graduated MA from Glasgow University in 1857. [NRS.GD1.32.38/14][RGG]

GRANT, JOHN, born7 May 1814, died in San Francisco, California, in September 1854. [Rosemarkie gravestone, Easter Ross]

GRANT, PETER, in Baltimore, Maryland, a letter to his father John Grant in Leith, in which he refers to 'the poor deluded

Highlanders who have gone to America', dated in 1803. [NRS,GD248.702.5]

GRANT, PETER, from Corarnstilmore, Fhearnasdail, Glen Feshie, Inverness-shire, emigrated in 1831 to Puslinch, Upper Canada, [HS.16.4.17]

GRANT, PETER GUILLAN, born on 21 January 1862 in Dundee, Angus, son of Reverend Peter Grant and his wife Helen Guillan, died in Victoria, British Columbia, on 16 May 1897. [F.5.329]

GRANT, or MILLIKEN, SARAH, in Missouri, heir to her father Thomas Milliken in Wallacetown, Ayr, and to her mother Rosina McTier or Milliken, on 26 August 1887. [NRS.S/H]

GRANT, W. C., in Oregon City, a letter re his travels in the United States and Canada, dated 1851. [NRS.NRAS.0770]

GREIG, JOHN, born 1781 in Scotland, settled in New York in 1799, died in Canandaiqua, New York, on 1 April 1858. [GM.ns.2/4.682]

GROVES, or REID, ANNIE, in USA, a Power of Attorney in favour of Sam. W. Radcliffe, dated 18 July 1865. [NRS.RD1240.117]

GUNN, JOHN, was born at Farr, Sutherland in 1806, was educated at King's College, Aberdeen, from 1825 until 1830, a missionary in Cape Breton, Nova Scotia, in 1838, minister at Broad Cove from 1840 until his death on 2 November 1870. [F.7.607]

GUNN, PATRICK JOSEPH, in Denver, Colorado, heir to his grandfather John Gunn, a spirit merchant in Glasgow, re property in Dunoon, Argyll, on 16 January 1889. [NRS.S/H]

HADDOW, SCOTT, and DALE, merchants in Glasgow, trading with New York and Demerara from 1819 to 1820. [NRS.CS96.3384]

HALKETT, JAMES BROOKE, in Ottawa, Ontario, heir to his grandmother Euphemia Wallace, wife of Samuel Halkett a brewer in Edinburgh, who died in December 1842, re property in St Andrews, Fife, 6 December 1889. [NRS.S/H]

HALL, GEORGE, in Brighton, Massachusetts, heir to his mother Mary Milne, widow of James Hall a merchant in Aberdeen, who died on 28 May 1890, 6 February 1900. [NRS.S/H]

HAMILTON, JOHN ROBERT, in New York, an inventory dated 1876. [NRS.SC70.179.66]

HAMILTON, PETER, from Monyguil, Arran, settled in Inverness township, Megantic County, Quebec, in 1831. [TNA.CO384.28.24-26]

HAMILTON, WILLIAM, from Cloined, Arran, settled in Inverness township, Megantic County, Quebec, in 1831. [TNA.CO384.28.24-26]

HAMILTON, WILLIAM, from Glenloig, Arran, settled in Inverness township, Megantic County, Quebec, in 1831. [TNA.CO384.28.24-26]

HAMILTON, WILLIAM DUNLOP, in Montreal, Quebec, a marriage contract with Frances W. Murdoch, dated 27 February 1863. [NRS.RD1174.1]

HAMILTON, WILLIAM, in Regina, Northwest Territories, Canada, was served heir to his mother Elizabeth Cameron or Hamilton in London who died on 8 March 1898. [NRS.S/H]

HARDIE, JAMES HENRY, in Derby, Connecticut, heir to his father William Keir Hardie, an engineer in Glasgow, who died on 14 July 1870, re property in Polmont, Stirlingshire, 14 January 1889. [NRS.S/H]

HARDING, GEORGE I., from America, graduated MD at Glasgow University in 1830. [RGG]

HARDMAN, JAMES, in Montreal, Quebec, an inventory dated 1876. [NRS.SC70.176.660]

HARGRAVES, JAMES, letters from Hudson Bay from 1847 until 1855.[NRS.GD1 380.1]

HARKNESS, Captain JAMES, born 1828, son of Gregor Harkness MD [1802-1853] and his wife Isabella Laurie [1804-1878], died in Galveston, Texas, on 17 August 1872. [Kilmun gravestone, Argyll]

HARLEY, THOMAS, a joiner in Kingston, Ontario, heir to his mother Margaret Dewar, wife of George Harley in Aberlady, East Lothian, who died on 21 December 1876, re property in Limekilns, Fife, on 15 July 1887. [NRS.S/H]

HARRIS, RUSSEL, from America, graduated MA from Marischal College in Aberdeen around 1765. [MCA]

HARTT, HENRY ALLINE, from America, graduated MD from Glasgow University in 1836. [RGG]

HASTIE, ADAM, born 1833, son of John and Mary Hastie, died in Syracuse, New York, on 12 February 1865. [Kirkpatrick Juxta gravestone, Dumfries-shire]

HENDERSON, R., a joiner from Lindores, Fife, emigrated to Canada in April 1883. [Fife Journal:21.4.1883]

HENDRY, Reverend DONALD, from Arran, settled in Inverness township, Megantic County, Quebec, in 1831. [TNA.CO384.28.24-26]

HENDERSON, JAMES, in New York bound for Brazil, letters from 1832 until 1855. [NRS.NRAS.0852]

HENDERSON, JOHN, in Louisiana, an inventory dated 1876. [NRS.SC70.179.857]

HENDERSON, WILLIAM, in Holyoke, Massachusetts, heir to his uncle William Henderson in Pultneytown, Wick, Caithness, who died on 27 July 1885, on 14 July 1891. [NRS.S/H]

HENDERSON, WILLIAM, in Chicago, Illinois, heir to his father George Henderson in Fife-Keith, who died on 7 December 1888, on 17 January 1891. [NRS.S/H]

HENRY, DONALD, from Corrygills, Arran, settled in Inverness township, Megantic County, Quebec, with a family of seven, in 1831. [TNA.CO384.28.24-26]

HENRY, EMMA, eldest daughter of Bernard Henry in Philadelphia, Pennsylvania, married George, eldest son of Lord Wood of the Court of Session in Edinburgh, in Philadelphia on 11 April 1846. [GM.ns.24.72]

HENRY, WILLIAM, from Arran, emigrated via Lamlash, Arran, aboard the brigantine Caledonia bound for Canada in 1829, landed in Quebec on 25 June 1829. [TNA.CO384.28.24/26]

HEPBURN, J., toured through America, to settle in Oregon, letters 1874 to 1875. [NRS.NRAS.1021]

HERALD, JAMES, son of John Herald a weaver in Kirriemuir, Angus, was educated at Marischal College in Aberdeen in 1845, later a Presbyterian minister in Canada. [MCA]

HERRIES, WILLIAM FERDINAND, graduated CM from Glasgow University in 1824. [RGG]

HEWAT, RICHARD ANDREW JAMES, in North Adams, Massachusetts, heir to his brother Thomas Hewat in Melrose, Selkirkshire, who died on 1 November 1899, re property in Galashiels, Selkirkshire, 10 April 1900. [NRS.S/H]

HILL, DAVID, a farmer in Fowler, Fresno, California, heir to his sister Isabella Matthewson Hill, wife of John Aiton a farmer there, who died on 10 November 1887, re land in Lochgelly, Fife, on 14 February 1889, [NRS.S/H]; a fruit grower in Anderson, California, heir to his father William Hill, a publican in Lochgelly, Fife, who died on 3 December 1869, on 5 May 1897. [NRS.S/H]

HILL, GEORGE, in Boston, USA, an inventory dated 1879. [NRS.SC70.195.430]

HILL, MIJSELL STODART, in Boston, USA, an inventory, dated 1878. [NRS.SC70.189.24]

HILL, WILLIAM, a Sunday school teacher in New York, a letter dated 1859. [NRS.NRAS.0744.4]

HOGG, ANDREW, in Jersey City, New Jersey, was served heir to his sister Jean Hogg, wife of John Miller in Highland Falls, New York, who died on 7 May 1879. [NRS.S/H]

HOGG, ROBERT, youngest brother of the Ettrick Shepherd, died on passage to North America on 24 June 1831. [GM.103.286]

HOME, FRANCIS EDWARD GEORGE, a farmer in Glassville, New Brunswick, was served heir to his uncle Reverend Frederick Home of Paddockmyre, residing in Carnoustie, Angus, who died on 17 October 1898, re land in Coldinghamlaw, Berwickshire. [NRS.S/H]

HOME, WILLIAM MURRAY, a grocer in Milwaukee, Wisconsin, heir to his brother James Home in Janesville, Wisconsin, who died on 15 June 1899, re property in Inverurie, Aberdeenshire, on 29 January 1900. [NRS.S/H]

HOOD, or TEMPLE, CHRISTINA, in Santa Rosa, California, heir to her grand-father James Hood a wright in Drybriggs, Cupar, Fife, who died on 7 October 1853. [NRS.S/H]

HOOD, JAMES, born 1834, from Dundee in Angus, a seaman aboard the Annie Jane of Liverpool bound from Liverpool with emigrants bound for Quebec, was shipwrecked off Vatersey in the Outer Hebrides in 1853 but survived. [WAJ]HOOD, JENNIE, in Los Guillicos Ranch, Santa Rosa, California, heir to her grand-father James Hood a wright in Drybriggs, Cupar, Fife, who died on 7 October 1853. [NRS.S/H]

HOOD, MARGARET, died in Quebec on 3 November 1861. [Dundee, Howff gravestone]

HOOD, or SHAW, MARY, in Wildwood Ranch, Santa Rosa, California, heir to her grand-father James Hood a wright in Drybriggs, Cupar, Fife, who died on 7 October 1853. [NRS.S/H]

HOPE, G. R., a letter from Nassau in the Bahamas in 1861, died in Honolulu, Hawaii, in 1882. [NRS.NRAS.1021]

HOPE, H.W., letter from California in 1861. [NRS.NRAS.1021]

HOSSACK, DONALD, from Skye, Inverness-shire, emigrated via Greenock aboard the Royal Adelaide bound for St John, New Brunswick, later to Fredericton, N.B., petitioned the New Brunswick House of Assembly in 1838. [PANB.RS24/4/77]

HOWAT, ALEXANDER K., in Canada West, a deed dated 12 July 1865. [NRS.1247.333]

HOWDEN, JOHN, in Toronto, Ontario, heir to his sister Isabella Grieve Howden in Edinburgh, who died on 21 March 1900, re property in Edinburgh, on 7 July 1900. [NRS.S/H]

HUGGINS, HENRY, in Mansfield, Ohio, an inventory dated 1878. [NRS.SC70.190.798]

HUGHES, ROBERT STEVENSON, in Oromocto, New Brunswick, heir to his mother Jane Ritchie Stevenson, widow of Hugh Hughes a shipmaster in Greenock, Renfrewshire, who died on 13 September 1890, re property in Greenock. [NRS.SH]

HUME, HENRY, in Charleston, South Carolina, heir to his brother William Hume, a bank agent in Partick, Glasgow, who died on 15 June 1877, re property in Falkirk, Stirlingshire, 29 March 1887. [NRS.S/H]

HUNTER, HUGH, in Rockbottom, Massachusetts, heir to his mother Janet Grant or Hunter at Broomhills, Largs, Ayrshire, who died on 5 September 1890, re property in Largs. [NRS.S/H]

HUNTER, JAMES, born 1849, died in Mobile, Alabama, on 31 January 1886. [St Andrews Cathedral gravestone, Fife]

HUNTER, JOHN ROBERT, in Los Angeles, California, heir to his uncle Robert Hunter manager of the Agra Bank in Edinburgh who died on 19 December 1890, on 11 June 1891. [NRS.S/H]

HUNTER, PATRICK, in Fort Scott, Kansas, heir to his grandfather Andrew Burns in Nottingham, England. [NRS.S/H]

HUNTER, TOMMY MORRIS, an infant, died in Darien, Georgia, on 15 May 1876. [St Andrews Cathedral gravestone, Fife]

HUTCHINSON, JOHN, born 1834, from Ayr, a seaman aboard the Annie Jane of Liverpool bound from Liverpool with emigrants bound for Quebec, was shipwrecked off Vatersey in the Outer Hebrides in 1853 but survived. [WAJ]

HUTTON, ANDREW, a teacher in Platteville, Wisconsin, heir to his father James Hutton in Badger, Wisconsin, who died on 5 July 1889, re property in Dunfermline. Fife, on 5 May 1890. [NRS.S/H.]

IMRIE, JAMES ROGER, a farmer in Tilsonbury, Ontario, heir to his brother Peter Imrie, a contractor in Innerleithen, Peeblesshire, who died on 14 June 1888, re property in West Lothian and Peeblesshire, on 12 April 1889. [NRS.S/H]

IMRIE, WILLIAM BECK, in Richmond, Quebec, an inventory dated 1876. [NRS.SC70.181.367]

INNES, ALEXANDER, son of Alexander Innes of Bridgend, Glen Livet, Banffshire, settled in America in 1840, a hotel keeper, died in Port Dover, Canada West on 17 April 1860. [GM.ns2.9.210]

IRELAND, ALEXANDER TAYLOR, born 1864, second son of Thomas Ireland in Crail, Fife, died in Brooklyn, New York, on 11 January 1886. [PJ] [EFR]

IRONSIDE, CATHERINE, born 1805 in New Deer, Aberdeenshire, daughter of William Ironside and his wife Margaret Alexander, married Daniel Lamont in 1835 in Whitby County, Ontario, died in 1876, a letter dated 1866. [ANESFHS]

IRONSIDE, MAGGIE ALLAN, born 1863, daughter of James Ironside born 1816, died 1875, and his wife Ann Tennant, born 1822, died 1916, died in California on 17 June 1889. [New Deer gravestone, Aberdeenshire]

IRVINE, ALEXANDER ECCLESTONE, a saddler in Philadelphia, Pennsylvania, heir to his father James Irvine, a merchant in

Lossiemouth, Moray, who died on 25 December 1883, on 21 January 1889. [NRS.S/H]

IRVING, EMMA, youngest daughter of Jacob Aemilius Irving of Bonshaw, Dumfries-shire, married Reverend Charles Gresford Edmondes, from Glamorgan, Wales, in Newmarket, Upper Canada, on 14 July 1866. [GM.ns3/2.398]

IRVING, J. T., in New York, correspondence with Edward Ellsworth in Fort Gibson, Arkansas, from 1835 until 1838. [NRS.NRAS.1239]

ISBISTER, JAMES, son of Thomas Isbister at the Red River in Canada, was educated at Marischal College in Aberdeen1n 1844, later a schoolmaster in Belhelvie, Aberdeenshire. [MCA]

ISBISTER, WILLIAM, of the Hudson Bay Company in 1830. [OA]

JAFFRAY, DAVID, a manufacturer in Irvine, Ayrshire, trading with Quebec, Demerara, and Tobago from 1808 to 1809. [cs96.2047]

JAMESON, JAMES, born 1843, son of James Jameson [1806-1895] and his wife Isabel Carnie [1822-1889], died in Barre, Vermont, on 7 May 1900. [Banchory Ternan gravestone, Aberdeenshire]

JAMIESON, ARCHIBALD, born 1820, from Fillaford, Sandness, Shetland Islands, a cook/seaman aboard the Annie Jane of Liverpool bound from Liverpool with emigrants bound for Quebec, was shipwrecked off Vatersey in the Outer Hebrides in 1853 but survived. [WAJ]

JARDINE, Commander WILLIAM, of the Royal Navy, son of Sir William Jardine of Applegirth, Dumfries-shire, married Louisa Archer Harvey, daughter of G. Cockburn Harvey, in Halifax, Nova Scotia, on 18 June 1864. [GM.ns2/17.234]

JELLY, WILLOUGHBY WAGNER, a hatter in Newark, New Jersey, heir to his uncle Thomas Aitkenhead Jelly in Ryde, Isle of Wight, England, who died on 26 February 1865, re property in Edinburgh. [NRS.S/H]

JENKINS, NESBIT H. B., in Texas, power of attorney to Cecil C. B. Jenkins, subscribed on 6 May 1864. [NRS.RD1228.236]

JOHNSON, Mrs CATHERINE, born in Scotland in 1773, died of old age in Fayetteville, North Carolina in November 1849. [FMS/NC]

JOHNSTON, DAVID HENRY, in Mehama, Oregon, was served heir to his mother Jane Sibbald, widow of George Johnston a manufacturer in East Wemyss, Fife, who died on 15 April 1898, re property at Royal Circus, Edinburgh. [NRS.S/H] JOHNSTONE, JOHN, born 1802, formerly a merchant in Elgin, Moray, an accountant with Hirchfield and Barnett, died at 6 Hamilton Avenue, Brooklyn, New York, of typhus fever on 28 February 1853. [IA]

JOHNSTON, ROBERT, and Company, merchants in Newfoundland, sederunt book from 1816 until 1817. [NRS.CS96.905.1]

JOHNSTON, THOMAS, in Peoria, Illinois, and California, letters from 1849 until 1850. [NRS.NRAS.0675]

KAY, DAVID, in America, Power of Attorney granted to Robert M. Kay, dated 28 October 1862. [NRS.RD1177.574]

KEAY, PATRICK, from Glasgow, was educated at King's College in Aberdeen in 1845, later a minister in Nashwaak, New Brunswick.
[KCA]

KEDDIE, THOMAS, a farmer in Huntsville, Kansas, heir to his mother Agnes Walkingshaw or Keddie in Maddiston who died on 6 November 1887, re lands of Maddiston, Muiravonside, Stirlingshire, on 12 March 1889. [NRS.S/H]

KELSO, ALEXANDER, with a family of eight persons, in North Sannox, Arran, bound via Lamlash aboard the brigantine <u>Caledonia</u> bound for Canada, in 1829, landed in Quebec on 25 June 1829. [TNA.CO384.22.3-5]

KELSO, ARCHIBALD, with a family of eight persons, in Glen, Arran, bound for Canada, 1829. [TNA.CO384.22.3-5]

KELSO, or MCKILLOP, CATHERINE, with a party of four persons, from Corrie, Arran, bound for Canada, 1829. [TNA.CO384.22.3-5]

KELSO, JOHN, from Corrie, Arran, settled in Inverness township, Megantic County, Quebec, in 1831. [TNA.CO384.28.24-26]

KELSO, or MCMILLAN, MARGARET, with a family of three persons, from Loggantwine, Arran, bound for Canada, 1829. [TNA.CO384.22.3-5]

KELSO, ROBERT, with a family of eight persons, from Loggantwine, Arran, bound via Lamlash aboard the brigantine Caledonia for Canada, in 1829, landed in Quebec on 25 June 1829. [TNA.CO384.22.3-5]

KELSO, WILLIAM, with a family of seven persons, from Mid Sannox, Arran, bound via Lamlash aboard the brigantine Caledonia for Canada, 1829, landed in Quebec on 25 June 1829. [TNA.CO384.22.3-5]

KENNEDY, AENEAS, third son of Reverend Angus Kennedy, the Free Church minister in Dornoch, Ross and Cromarty, died in Hamilton, Canada West, on 7 November 1854. [IA]

KENNEDY, CHARLES P., youngest son of Reverend Angus Kennedy, the Free Church minister in Dornoch, Ross and Cromarty, died in New Dundee, Canada West, on 25 April 1853. [IA]

KENNEDY, GEORGE, in Cherry Villa, Ontario, heir to his great great grandfather Daniel Shaw, a weaver in Maxwellton, Paisley, Renfrewshire, who died in 1837, re property in Paisley, on 21 May 1889. [NRS.S/H]

KENNEDY, JOHN, from Knockanbuie, Fhearnasdail, Glen Feshie, Inverness-shire, emigrated in 1831 to Puslinch, Upper Canada, [HS.16.4.17]

KENNEDY, Reverend ROBERT, in Cheltenham, Canada, an inventory dated 1874. [NRS.SC70.166.638]

KENNEDY, WILLIAM, with eight children, from Knockanbuie, Fhearnasdail, Glen Feshie, Inverness-shire, emigrated in 1833 to Puslinch, Upper Canada, [HS.16.4.17]

KENT, ROBERT, a blacksmith in Brooklyn, New York, heir to his father Robert Kent, a carter in Bothwell, Lanarkshire, who died on 7 January 1880. [NRS.S/H]

KENT, WILLIAM RALPH, in Ottawa, Ontario, an inventory dated 1876. [NRS.SC70.181.261]

KERR, JOHN, born 29 August 1815 in Dalry, Ayrshire, son of Hugh Kerr and his wife Jane Boyle, emigrated to USA in 1841, settled as a joiner and farmer in Paddock's Grove, Maddison County, Illinois, returned to Dalry in 1853. [NLS letter]

KERR, JOHN, from Urnbeg, Arran, settled in Inverness township, Megantic County, Quebec, in 1831. [TNA.CO384.28.24-26]

KILMARNOCK, Lord, son of the Countess of Errol, died in Montreal, Quebec, on 7 February 1852. [GM.ns37.399]

KINCAID, MARGARET, daughter of the late Thomas Kincaid, a merchant in Leith, married Alexander Rowand, MD in Montreal, Quebec, in Edinburgh on 25 January 1844. [GM.ns.21.309]

KING, WILLIAM, at Lake Nipissine, Callander, Canada West, heir to his brother James King, a labourer in Dunblane, Stirlingshire, who ied on 30 August 1889. [NRS.S/H]

KINNEAR, DAVID, born 1807 in Edinburgh, Proprietor of the 'Montreal Herald', died in Montreal, Quebec, on 20 November 1862. [GM.ns2/14.127]

KINNEAR, ISABELLA, from Fife, died in Hoboken, New York, on 1 July 1884. [S.12796]

KIRKWOOD, JOHN, in Chicago, Illinois, an inventory dated 1873. [NRS.SC70.160.562]

KNOX, WILLIAM, possibly from Selkirk, emigrated, with his family, via Liverpool aboard the Republic bound for New York in 1838, a letter. [NRS.GD1.813.15]

LACHLAN, Captain J. M., General Manager of the U.S. and Brazil Steamship Company letters to Sir William MacKinnon, dated 1888-1891. [NRS.NRAS.0323]

LAING, ANDREW, in Black Diamond, Pennsylvania, heir to Andrew Laing, a collier in New Gilston, Fife, who died on 25 January 1854, on 5 April 1900. [NRS.S/H]

LAING, ARNOLD MAXWELL, infant son of S.J. Anderson in Toledo, Ohio, died in 1899. [S.17351]

LAING, GEORGE, in Hamilton, Canada, an inventory dated 1872. [NRS.SC70.157.1013]

LAING, GRACE, daughter of S.J. Anderson in Toledo, Ohio, died on 28 December 1898. [S.17339]

LAING, JOHN, born 1893 son of S.J. Anderson in Toledo, Ohio, died on 3 January 1899. [S.17339]

LAING, RUTH JANETTA, born 1896, second daughter of S.J. Anderson in Toledo, Ohio, died on 8 January 1899. [S.17351]

LAIRD, JAMES NICHOLSON, in Hamilton, Ontario, heir to his sister Marianne Laird in St Margaret's Hope, South Ronaldsay, Orkney, who died on 14 April 1900, on 10 September 1900, re property there. [NRS.S/H]

LAMB, JAMES, from Fordell and Pathead, Fife, died at the home of his son-in-law R. P. Strathearn, in Senega, Ventura Valley, California on 12 November 1884. [S.12946]

LAMON, ISABELLA, born in Scotland in 1802, wife of A. McDonald, died in Mississippi on 17 January 1864. [Carolina church, Mishoba County, Mississippi]

LAMONT, FLETCHER, in St Louis, USA, an inventory dated 1875. [NRS.SC70.172.748]

LANG, ARTHUR FORREST, in Highland, Jacksonville, Florida, heir to his father Arthur Lang in Ayr who died on 18 August 1890. [NRS.S/H]

LAWSON, GEORGE, born 1814, son of James Lawson [1769-1827], and his wife Elizabeth Smart, was drowned off Newfoundland on 26 April 1832. [Constitution Road gravestone, Dundee]

LAWSON, or WATERSTONE, ISABELLA, in New Stratsville, Ohio, heir to her mother Helen Clark or Waterstone in Lasswade, Midlothian, who died on 24 December 1886, 6 June 1887. [NRS.S/H]

LAWSON, JAMES, born 9 November 1799 in Glasgow, eldest son of James Lawson a merchant, matriculated at Glasgow University in 1812, emigrated to USA in 1815, a writer, journalist, poet and insurance broker in New York, died in Yonkers, New York, on 20 March 1880. [RGG]

LEIGHTON, THOMAS, in East Cambridge, Boston, letters from 1838 until 1848. [NRS.NRAS.1200]

LENNOX, GEORGE, a potter from Portobello near Edinburgh, an emigrant aboard the Annie Jane of Liverpool, master William Mason, bound from Liverpool to Quebec, was shipwrecked but survived near Vatersay in the Outer Hebrides on 28 September 1853. [WAJ]

LESLIE, ALEXANDER, in Montreal, Quebec, letters from 1827 until 1830. [NRS.NRAS.1081]

LILLIE, SUSAN, wife of Adam Pearson, from 22 Blackford Road, Edinburgh, died in Fordham, New York, on 21 August 1884. [S.12838]

LINDSAY, ALEXANDER, in New York, was served heir to his brother John Lindsay in Dundee, Angus, who died 12 December 1898. [NRS.S/H]

LINDSAY, JAMES MACDONALD MACLEOD, a clerk in Toronto, Canada, was served heir to his brother William Lindsay, in Tuckersmith, Ontario, who died on 19 November 1865. [NRS.S/H]

LINDSAY, THOMAS, an express vanman in New Westminster, British Columbia, heir to his father John Lindsay in Clepington, Dundee, who died 24 February 1890, 12 September 1890. [NRS.S/H.]

LINDSAY, WILLIAM, born 1843, youngest son of Robert Lindsay in Edinburgh, a typefounder in Chicago who died in Brooklyn, New York, on 27 April 1885. [S.13057]

LIVESEY, THOMAS JOHN, in Pueblo, Colorado, heir to his father John Livesey in Blackburn, Lancashire, who died on 8 August 1886, re property in Inverness, on 3 November 1887. [NRS.S/H]

LOGAN, Sir EDWARD, in Canada, an inventory dated 1875. [NRS.SC70.175.432]

LOGAN, FRANCIS, with a family of six persons, from North Sannox, Arran, bound for Canada, in 1829. [TNA.CO384.22.3/5]

LOTHIAN, GEORGE SHARP, in Chicago, Illinois, heir to his father George Lothian in Edinburgh, who died on 12 January 1900, re property there, on 3 May 1900. [NRS.S/H]

LOWDOUN, GEORGE, a cloth merchant in Glasgow, trading with Jamaica, Martinique, New York and San Domingo between 1819 and 1821. [NRS.CS16.768]

LUMSDEN, THOMAS HENRY, in Memphis, Tennessee, was served heir to his father John McVeigh Lumsden of Belhelvie Lodge, Aberdeenshire, residing in Galt, Canada, who died on 27 September 1898. [NRS.S/H]

MCADAM, QUINTIN, son of Alexander McAdam of Grinnet, Ayrshire, died at Canandarque, USA, on 18 October 1853. [IA]

MCALISTER, CHARLES, born in Scotland in 1777, a farmer, died in Fayetteville District, North Carolina, of consumption in December 1849. [FMS/NC]

MACALISTER, KATHERINE ELISABETH, daughter of A. MacAlister of Torrisdale Castle, Highland, married William Rose, eldest son of John Rose in Montreal, Quebec, there on 2 January 1868. [GM.ns3.5.385]

MCALLAN, DUGALD, from Lochranza, Arran, settled in Inverness township, Megantic County, Quebec, in 1831. [TNA.CO384.28.24-26]

MCARTHUR, ALEXANDER, born 1843 in Nairn, emigrated to Canada in 1861, a banker in Toronto, Ontario, from 1861 until 1864, an employee of the Hudson Bay Company from 1864 to 1868, settled in Winnipeg in 1869, manager of the Manitoba Investment Association, died in 1887. [NLS]

MCASKILL, ARCHIBALD, born 1832, from North Uist, Outer Hebrides, bound via Greenock aboard the Waterhen of London to Quebec in 1849. [NRS.GD221.4435]

MCAULAY, ARCHIBALD, born 1814, with Catherine McAulay born 1821, and Margaret McAulay born 1847, from North Uist, Outer Hebrides, bound via Greenock aboard the Waterhen of London to Quebec in 1849. [NRS.GD221.4435]

MACAULAY, W. A., at Guelph, Ontario, a letter, 1890s. [SRA.TD1]

MCBAIN, ALEXANDER, and his wife Catherine, possibly from Kandow, Fhearnasdail, Glen Feshie, Inverness-shire, emigrated in 1831 to Puslinch, Upper Canada, [HS.16.4.17]

MCBEAN, JOHN, born 1845, son of David McBean, tacksman of the Mains of Flowerburn, and his wife Isabella, died at Stonewall, Indian Territory, USA, on 31 December 1901. [Rosemarkie gravestone, Easter Ross]

MCBEATH, ADAM, son of Neil McBeath [1807-1873] and his wife Margaret Rose [1813-1867], died in Toronto, Canada, in 1880. [Clyne Kirkton gravestone, Sutherland]

MCBEATH, JOHN, son of Neil McBeath [1807-1873] and his wife Margaret Rose [1813-1867], died in Toronto, Canada, in 1888. [Clyne Kirkton gravestone, Sutherland]

MCBEATH, ……, son of Morrison McBeath of St Francis Xavier, was born in Winnipeg, Manitoba, on 25 June 1884. [S.12799]

MCCALLIE, DAVID, from Whithorn in Galloway, later in Boston, Massachusetts, a sasine dated 1894. [NRS.RS.Whithorn.7.153.191)

MCCALLUM, ROBERT, in Preston, Minnesota, an inventory dated 1876. [NRS.SC70.176.834]

MCCAW, WILLIAM, son of Robert McCaw [1817-1876] and his wife Jessie McTier, [1820-1901], died in Illinois aged 68. [Colmonell gravestone, Ayrshire]

MCCOLL, ARCHIBALD, from Nova Scotia, graduated MD from Glasgow University in 1836. [RGG]

MCCOLL, HUGH, in New York, an inventory dated 1876. [NRS.SC70.178.86]

MCCORMICK, EMMELINE LECKIE, daughter of James McCormick a Lieutenant in the United States Navy, was granted part of the lands of Drumoyne in Scotland on 23 March 1857. [RGS.258.27.69]

MCCOSH, JAMES, born 1 April 1811 in Carskeoch, died in Princeton, New Jersey, on 16 November 1894. [Straiton gravestone, Ayrshire]

MCCOURT, JAMES, in Philadelphia, Pennsylvania, graduated CM from Glasgow University in 1839. [CMM]

MCCUAIG, RORY, from Skye, emigrated via Greenock aboard the Royal Adelaide bound for St John, New Brunswick, later to Fredericton, N.B., petitioned the New Brunswick House of Assembly in 1838. [PANB.RS24/4/77]

MCDAVID, JAMES, born 1873, a divinity student at Glasgow University, fifth son of James McDavid in Newton Stewart, Dumfries, died in Buffalo, New York, on 4 January 1899. [S.7334]

MCDERMID, ARCHIBALD, settled in Reach, Ontario, by 1848, a petitioner. [NRS.GD112.61.5]

MCDERMID, COLIN, settled in Reach, Ontario, by 1848, a petitioner. [NRS.GD112.61.5]

MCDERMID, JOHN, settled in Reach, Ontario, by 1848, a petitioner. [NRS.GD112.61.5]

MCDIARMID, ALEXANDER, born 1825, from North Uist, Outer Hebrides, bound via Greenock aboard the Waterhen of London to Quebec in 1849. [NRS.GD221.4435]

MCDONALD, ALEXANDER, born 1804, with Isobel McDonald born 1803, James McDonald born 1829, Ian McDonald born 1831, Angus McDonald born 1833, Alexander McDonald born 1838, from North Uist, Outer Hebrides, bound via Greenock aboard the Waterhen of London to Quebec in 1849. [NRS.GD221.4435]

MCDONALD, ALEXANDER, born 1779, with Flora McDonald born 1789, Donald McDonald born 1821, Margaret McDonald born 1823, Flora McDonald born 1825, John McDonald born 1826,

Marion McDonald born 1827, Ann McDonald born 1829, from North Uist, Outer Hebrides, bound via Greenock aboard the Waterhen of London to Quebec in 1849. [NRS.GD221.4435]

MCDONALD, ALEXANDER, born 1799, with Catherine McDonald born 1812, Allan McDonald born 1823, Donald McDonald born 1826, Roderick McDonald born 1830, Archibald McDonald born 1831, John McDonald born 1834, Margaret McDonald born 1837, Christy McDonald born 1843, Marion McDonald born 1848, from North Uist, Outer Hebrides, bound via Greenock aboard the Waterhen of London to Quebec in 1849. [NRS.GD221.4435]

MCDONALD, ALLAN, from Skye, Inverness-shire, emigrated via Greenock aboard the Royal Adelaide bound for St John, New Brunswick, later to Fredericton, N.B., petitioned the New Brunswick House of Assembly in 1838. [PANB.RS24/4/77]

MCDONALD, ALEXANDER, born 1830, from North Uist, Outer Hebrides, bound via Greenock aboard the Waterhen of London to Quebec in 1849. [NRS.GD221.4435]

MCDONALD, ANGUS, born 1815, from North Uist, Outer Hebrides, bound via Greenock aboard the Waterhen of London to Quebec in 1849. [NRS.GD221.4435]

MCDONALD, ANGUS, emigrated via Stornaway, Lewis, settled in Manitoba by 1888, [two letters published in The Scotsman dated 21 September 1888].

MACDONALD, AUSTIN, from Skye, Inverness-shire, emigrated via Greenock aboard the Royal Adelaide bound for St John, New Brunswick, later to Fredericton, N.B., petitioned the New Brunswick House of Assembly in 1838. [PANB.RS24/4/77]

MACDONALD, Reverend Dr A. C., born 1830, formerly minister of the Free Church in Queen Street, Inverness, emigrated via Liverpool aboard the Lake Huron bound for Halifax, Nova Scotia, on 26 March 1898, landed there on 6 April 1808, later in Klondike. [TGSI.70.59]

MCDONALD, CHRISTIAN, born 1821, from North Uist, Outer Hebrides, bound via Greenock aboard the Waterhen of London to Quebec in 1849. [NRS.GD221.4435]

MCDONALD, DONALD, from Glaister, Arran, settled in Inverness township, Megantic County, Quebec, in 1831. [TNA.CO384.28.24-26]

MCDONALD, JOHN, from Skye, Inverness-shire, a merchant in Alabama, New York, South Carolina, Florida and Georgia, letters from 1840 until 1878. [NRS.NRAS.116]

MCDONALD, DONALD, born 1826 from North Uist, Outer Hebrides, bound via Greenock aboard the Waterhen of London to Quebec in 1849. [NRS.GD221.4435]

MCDONALD, DONALD, born 1799, with Catherine McDonald born 1799, Roderick McDonald born 1825, Donald McDonald born 1829, from North Uist, Outer Hebrides, bound via Greenock aboard the Waterhen of London to Quebec in 1849. [NRS.GD221.4435]

MCDONALD, DONALD, born 1821, from North Uist, Outer Hebrides, bound via Greenock aboard the Waterhen of London to Quebec in 1849. [NRS.GD221.4435]

MCDONALD, HUGH, from Skye, Inverness-shire, emigrated via Greenock aboard the Royal Adelaide bound for St John, New Brunswick, later to Fredericton, N.B., petitioned the New Brunswick House of Assembly in 1838. [PANB.RS24/4/77]

MCDONALD, JOHN, born 1823, from North Uist, Outer Hebrides, bound via Greenock aboard the Waterhen of London to Quebec in 1849. [NRS.GD221.4435]

MCDONALD, JOHN, born 1803, with Mary McDonald born 1804, Catherine McDonald born 1827, Christy McDonald born 1830, Duncan McDonald born 1833, Mary McDonald born 1834, Jonathan McDonald born 1836, John McDonald born 1838, Ann McDonald born 1840, Ann McDonald born 1842, from North Uist, Outer Hebrides, bound via Greenock aboard the Waterhen of London to Quebec in 1849. [NRS.GD221.4435]

MCDONALD, MARY, daughter of William McDonald a builder in Thurso, Caithness, married John Hardie, in Brooklyn, New York, on 18 July 1884. [S.12811]

MACDONALD, NEIL, born 1857, second son of Murdoch MacDonald clerk of works in Stornaway, Lewis, died at sea on 19 October 1883 on return voyage from San Francisco, California. [Old Sandwick gravestone, Stornaway.]

MCDONALD, RODERICK, born 1829, from North Uist, Outer Hebrides, bound via Greenock aboard the Waterhen of London to Quebec in 1849. [NRS.GD221.4435]

MCDONALD, ROD, born 1817, with Euphemia McDonald born 1823, John McDonald born 1848, Janet McDonald born 1823, from North Uist, Outer Hebrides, bound via Greenock aboard the Waterhen of London to Quebec in 1849. [NRS.GD221.4435]

MCDONALD, RONALD, born 1809, with his wife Marion born 1811, and children Ann born 1835, Kitty born 1836, Duncan born 1839, Mary born 1842, Neil born 1846, and Peggy born 1846, from North Uist, Outer Hebrides, emigrated via Greenock aboard the Cashmere of Glasgow bound for Quebec in 1849. [NRS.GD221.4011.53]

MCDONALD, RONALD, born 1820, from North Uist, Outer Hebrides, bound via Greenock aboard the Waterhen of London to Quebec in 1849. [NRS.GD221.4435]

MACDONALD, WALTER, a barrister, died in Hamilton, Ontario, on 10 January 1899. [S.17333]

MCDONALD, WILLIAM, from Skye, Inverness-shire, a merchant in Alabama, New York, South Carolina, Florida and Georgia, letters from 1840 until 1878. [NRS.NRAS.116]

MCDONALD, WILLIAM, born 1827, from North Uist, Outer Hebrides, bound via Greenock aboard the Waterhen of London to Quebec in 1849. [NRS.GD221.4435]

MCDONALD, Mrs, a widow, from Skye, Inverness-shire, emigrated via Greenock aboard the Royal Adelaide bound for St John, New Brunswick, later to Fredericton, N.B., petitioned the New Brunswick House of Assembly in 1838. [PANB.RS24/4/77]

MCDONELL, ANGUS, from Skye, Inverness-shire, emigrated via Greenock aboard the Royal Adelaide bound for St John, New Brunswick, later to Fredericton, N.B., petitioned the New Brunswick House of Assembly in 1838. [PANB.RS24/4/77]

MCDONELL, RANALD, from Skye, Inverness-shire, emigrated via Greenock aboard the Royal Adelaide bound for St John, New Brunswick, later to Fredericton, N.B., petitioned the New Brunswick House of Assembly in 1838. [PANB.RS24/4/77]

MCDONELL, WILLIAM, born 1826, from North Uist, Outer Hebrides, bound via Greenock aboard the Waterhen of London to Quebec in 1849. [NRS.GD221.4435]

MCDOUALL, ALLAN, born 1829, from North Uist, Outer Hebrides, bound via Greenock aboard the Waterhen of London to Quebec in 1849. [NRS.GD221.4435]

MCDOUALL, WILLIAM, born 1829, from North Uist, Outer Hebrides, bound via Greenock aboard the Waterhen of London to Quebec in 1849. [NRS.GD221.4435]

MCDOUGALD, ARCHIBALD, from Skye, Inverness-shire, emigrated via Greenock aboard the Royal Adelaide bound for St John, New Brunswick, later to Fredericton, N.B., petitioned the New Brunswick House of Assembly in 1838. [PANB.RS24/4/77]

MCDOUGALL, DONALD, from Skye, Inverness-shire, emigrated via Greenock aboard the Royal Adelaide bound for St John, New Brunswick, later to Fredericton, N.B., petitioned the New Brunswick House of Assembly in 1838. [PANB.RS24/4/77]

MCDOUGALL, DUNCAN, from Skye, Inverness-shire, emigrated via Greenock aboard the Royal Adelaide bound for St John, New Brunswick, later to Fredericton, N.B., petitioned the New Brunswick House of Assembly in 1838. [PANB.RS24/4/77]

MCDOUGALL, F.D., in Maryville, California, a letter dated 1857. [NRS.NRAS.0853]

MCDOUGALL, JOHN WRIGHT, in Toronto, Ontario, heir to his father Reverend John McDougall of Orchill, Braco, who died on 20 October 1888, re property in Glasgow, 27 September 1889, [NRS.S/H]

MCDOUGAL, NEIL, born 1787, with Ann McDougal born 1795, William McDougal born 1818, Mary McDougal born 1830, John McDougal born 1832, Archibald McDougal born 1839, Margaret McDougal born 1840, Mary McDougal born 1843, from North Uist, Outer Hebrides, bound via Greenock aboard the Waterhen of London to Quebec in 1849. [NRS.GD221.4435]

MCDOUGALL, NEILL, in So'bridge, Massachusetts, an inventory dated 1876. [NRS.SC70.178.480]

MCDOWELL, DAY H. in Prince Albert, North-West Territory, a Deed of Factory and Commission with Mary McDowell, in 1882. [NRS.RD.1884.323.332]

MACDUFF, WILLIAM, a clerk in New York, was served heir to his father Andrew MacDuff in Edinburgh on 19 July 1898, re property in Huntly Street, Edinburgh. [NSR.S/H]

MCEDWARD, or CLARK, CATHERINE, with her son Angus Clark, Fhearnasdail, Glen Feshie, Inverness-shire, emigrated in 1833 to Puslinch, Upper Canada, [HS.16.4.17]

MCEDWARD, DUNCAN, with his wife and seven children, from Glen Feshie, Inverness-shire, emigrated in 1831 to Puslinch, Upper Canada, [HS.16.4.17]

MCELROY, JANET, in New York, an inventory dated 1872.
[NRS.SC70.158.502]

MCEWAN, or OATES, born 1821, from the Isle of Lewis, with
Margaret Oates born 1853 in Haddington, East Lothian, emigrants
aboard the Annie Jane of Liverpool, master William Mason, bound
from Liverpool to Quebec, was shipwrecked and drowned near
Vatersay in the Outer Hebrides on 28 September 1853. [WAJ]

MACFARLANE, GEORGE, in Austerlitz, Columbia
County, New York, father of a son born on 1 August 1884.
[S.12819]

MCGILLIVRAY, CHARLES, from Skye, Inverness-shire,
emigrated via Greenock aboard the Royal Adelaide bound
for St John, New Brunswick, later to Fredericton, petitioned
the New Brunswick House of Assembly in 1838.
[PANB.RS24/4/77]

MCGILLIVRAY, DONALD, senior, from Skye, Inverness-
shire, emigrated via Greenock aboard the Royal Adelaide
bound for St John, New Brunswick, later to Fredericton, N.B.
petitioned the New Brunswick House of Assembly in 1838.
[PANB.RS24/4/77]

MCGILLIVRAY, DONALD, junior, from Skye, Inverness-
shire, emigrated via Greenock aboard the Royal Adelaide
bound for St John, New Brunswick, later to Fredericton,
N.B., petitioned the New Brunswick House of Assembly in
1838. [PANB.RS24/4/77]

MCGILLIVRAY, WILLIAM, from Egilsay in the Orkney
Islands, settled in America before 1857, letters.
[OA.GB241.D1.961]

MCGLASHAN, ALEXANDER, born 1795, with Janet McGlashan
born 1796, John McGlashan born 1825, Angus born 1827,
Alexander McGlashan born 1829, Donald McGlashan born
1831,Lachland McGlashan born 1833, Donald McGlashan born

1836, Mary McGlashan born 1836, Catherine McGlashan born 1839, from North Uist, Outer Hebrides, bound via Greenock aboard the Waterhen of London to Quebec in 1849. [NRS.GD221.4435]

MCGLASHAN, DONALD, born 1787, with his wife Catherine born 1807, and children Angus born 1833, Alexander born 1835, Ann born 1837, Flora born 1839, Donald born 1841, and Neil born 1848, from North Uist, Outer Hebrides, emigrated via Greenock, Renfrewshire, aboard the Cashmore of Glasgow bound for Quebec in 1849. [NRS.GD221.4011.53]

MCGLASHAN, NEIL, born 1790, with his wife Euphemia born 1791, and children Ewen born 1826, Ann born 1828, Christy born 1831. Alexander born 1836, Allan born 1838, Donald born 1840, and Mary born 1842, from North Uist, Outer Hebrides, emigrated via Greenock aboard the Cashmere of Glasgow bound for Quebec in 1849. [NRS.GD2214011.53]

MCGREGOR, CHARLES, in Leith, Midlothian, late from New York, a deed in 1882. [NRS.RD.1852.334.82]

MCGREGOR, JOHN, born 1807, from North Uist, Outer Hebrides, bound via Greenock aboard the Waterhen of London to Quebec in 1849. [NRS.GD221.4435]

MCGREGOR, JOHN, in Visalia, California, an inventory in 1876. [NRS.SC70.179.309]

MCGREGOR, Mrs MAY, born 1829, daughter of Colin Shanks a baker in Chapel Street, Aberdeen, and wife of William McGregor from Aberdeen, died in Walkerville, Ontario, on 1 May 1874. [AJ.27.5.1874]

MCHATTIE, ANNE, daughter of John McHattie a merchant in Aberdeen, and wife of Reverend John Tawse, died at the Manse of King, Upper Canada, on 22 June 1841. [AJ]

MCILWRAITH, JOHN, born 1808, was drowned off New York on 12 August 1845. [Barr gravestone, Ayrshire]

MCILWRICK, DAVID, born 1814, son of David McIlwrick in Altercannoch, [1764-1832] and his wife Helen McMurray, [1789-1852], died in Knoxville, USA, on 21 April 1844. [Colmonell gravestone, Ayrshire]

MCINNES, ANDREW, in Canada West, a deed dated 30 October 1865. [NRS.RD1247.625]

MCINNIS, ANGUS, born in Scotland in 1786, a farmer who died of pains in Fayetteville, North Carolina, in October 1849. [FMS/NC]

MCINNES, LACHLAN, born 1805, with his wife Marion born 1813, and children Donald born 1837, Flora born 1839, Finlay born 1841, John born 1843, Donald born 1845, and Christy born 1846, from North Uist, Outer Hebrides, emigrated via Greenock aboard the Cashmere of Glasgow bound for Quebec in 1849 in 1889. [NRS.GD2214011.53]

MCINNES, RONALD, born 1809, with Marion McInnes born 1814, Finlay McInnes born 1843, Angus McInnes born 1826, from North Uist, Outer Hebrides, bound via Greenock aboard the Waterhen of London to Quebec in 1849. [NRS.GD221.4435]

MCINROY, PATRICK, born 16 July 1845, younger son of James McInroy of Lude, Perthshire, died in Pueblo, Colorado, 12 November 1882. [Kilmaveonaig gravestone, Perthshire]

MCINROY, HENRY, born 1841, 5th son of James McInroy of Lude, Perthshire, died in Colorado on 12 June 1902, [Ilavenil gravestone, Perthshire]

MCINTOSH, DONALD, of Holyoke, Massachusetts, a deed of attorney with William McMichael, dated 1882. [NRS.1882.224.315]

MCINTOSH, JOHN, born 1784 in Marnoch, died in Sherbrook on St Mary's River, Nova Scotia, on 18 October 1858. [AJ.1.12.1858]

MCINTOSH, ROBERT, MD in California, a deed of attorney with John O. McKenzie, dated 1882. [NRS.1882.224.315]

MCINTYRE, ANDREW, from Sidderie, Arran, settled in Inverness township, Megantic County, Quebec, in 1831. [TNA.CO384.28.24-26]

MCINTYRE, DONALD, with a family of six persons, from Slidderie, Arran, bound for Canada, 1829. [TNA.CO384.22.3-5]

MCINTYRE, DONALD, a surgeon of the 43rd Regiment of Foot in America 1781, Inspector General of Hospitals in the Leeward Islands in 1796, graduated MD in 1803, died on 28 November 1815. [SAU]

MCINTYRE, NORMAN, born 1809, with Mary McIntyre born 1809, Innes McIntyre born 1834, Marion McIntyre born 1837, Peggy McIntyre born 1839, from North Uist, Outer Hebrides, bound via Greenock aboard the Waterhen of London to Quebec in 1849. [NRS.GD221.4435]

MCIVER, COLIN, born 1784 in Scotland, a married preacher, died of consumption in Fayetteville, North Carolina, in January 1850. [FMS/NC]

MCKANDY, JAMES, born 1845 in Aberdeen, late of the 78th Highlanders, died in Canada on 12 May 1880. [AJ]

MACKAY, ANNIE, born 1839, daughter of Hector Mackay in Strath, [1802-1861] and his wife Margaret Mackay, [1812-1890], died in Nevada, USA, in 1926. [Skerray gravestone, Sutherland]

MACKAY, DONALD, born 19 February 1829 in Creich, Sutherland, son of Aeneas Mackay and his wife Jane Urquhart, was educated at the University of St Andrews, a schoolmaster in Ullapool 1848-1853, a minister at Stoer, Sutherland, 1854 to 1876, minister at Gareloch, Nova Scotia 1876 -1882, then at Metiss, Quebec, 1884-1886, returned to Scotland, minister of the Gaelic Chapel in Rothesay 1888-1807, died on 9 November 1910. [F.3.182]

MACKAY, ETHEL REAY, born 1879, only child of John Mackay, died in Washington, USA, on 10 January 1898. [S.17037]

MACKAY, JAMES, in Warren, Ohio, was served heir to his uncle Alexander Mackay in Largs, Ayrshire, who died on 8 May 1880, re property in Chapelhall, Bothwell, Lanarkshire. [NRS.S/H]

MACKAY, JAMES DRUMMOND, in Toronto, Ontario, heir to his grandmother Elizabeth Gibb, wife of James Drummond a merchant in Stirling, who died on 9 June 1879, re property in Bothwell, Lanarkshire, on 17 June 1889. [NRS.S/H]

MACKAY, JAMES, son of John Mackay, [1818-1897], and his wife Anne Mackay in Achneskich, a contractor in St Louis, USA, husband of Jessie, parents of John, Angus, Ann and Jessie. [BM.269]

MACKAY, JOHN, son of John McKay a farmer in the Kirkton of Durris, in Kincardineshire, formerly of the Glengarry Infantry, died in Upper Canada on 4 March 1840. [AJ]

MACKAY, JOHN, ship carpenter, died in New York 1888, husband of Isabella Gunn died in Stornaway, Outer Hebrides, 1925. [Old Sandwick gravestone]

MACKAY, JOHN, father of Ethel Reay Mackay, born 1879, died in Washington on 10 January 1898. [S.17037]

MACKAY, MARY A., wife of William Brough, died in Brooklyn, New York, on 18 August 1884. [S.12841]

MCKAY, NEIL, born 1822, from Lewis, Outer Hebrides, died 1904, husband of Christina Rose, born 1826, from Loch Broom, Wester Ross, died 1897. [Gould Pioneer Cemetery, Lingwick, Quebec]

MACKAY, ROBERT OSBORNE, a wharfinger in Hamilton, Ontario, heir to his granduncle John Urquhart, a merchant in Bonar Bridge, Sutherland, who died 14 October 1888, re property in Bonar Bridge, on 25 January 1889. [NRS.S/H]

MACKAY, SARAH, daughter of Alexander Mackay at the Mill of Hole in Midmar, Aberdeenshire, died in Renfrew, Canada, on 23 July 1872. [AJ]

MCKEAGAN, ALEXANDER, born 1790, with Mary McKeagan born 1791, Angus McKeagan born 1824, John McKeagan born 1829, from North Uist, Outer Hebrides, bound via Greenock aboard the Waterhen of London to Quebec in 1849. [NRS.GD221.4435]

MCKEAN, JOHN, in Salt Lake City, Utah, heir to his uncle Hugh Crail Clark, a merchant in Denny, Stirlingshire, who died on 27 June 1892, re property in Newburgh, Fife, on 28 September 1900. [NRS.S/H]

MCKEARY, JOHN, born 1789, with Christy McKeary born 1799, Christy born 1822, Ann McKeary born 1830, Alexander McKeary born 1832, Archibald McKeary born 1834, Catherine McKeary born 1842, from North Uist, Outer Hebrides, bound via Greenock aboard the Waterhen of London to Quebec in 1849. [NRS.GD221.4435]

MCKECHNIE, JESSIE, born 1817, from Kiln Lane, Paisley, Renfrewshire, with her children Catherine McKechnie born 1840, Mary McKechnie born 1842, Jessie McKechnie born 1844, Eliza McKechnie born 1848, and Malcolm McKechnie born 1851, emigrants aboard the Annie Jane of Liverpool, master William Mason, bound from Liverpool to Quebec, was shipwrecked and drowned near Vatersay in the Outer Hebrides on 28 September 1853. [WAJ]

MCKECHNIE, STUART, eldest son of A. McKechnie, in St Austine [?], Fife, died on Canada West, on 5 May 1853. [GM.ns40.98]

MCKELVIE, DUNCAN, emigrated from Knockew, Arran, aboard the Caledonia in 1829, settled in Inverness township, Megantic County, Quebec, in 1831. [TNA.CO384.28.24-26]

MCKENZIE, ANDREW, born 1795, with Mary McKenzie born 1799, Euphemia McKenzie born 1827, Elspet McKenzie born 1829, John McKenzie born 1830, James McKenzie born 1833, Archibald McKenzie born 1836, from North Uist, Outer Hebrides, bound via Greenock aboard the Waterhen of London to Quebec in 1849. [NRS.GD221.4435]

MCKENZIE, ARCHIBALD, with a family of two persons, from Mid Arran, Buteshire, aboard the Caledonia in 1829, settled in Inverness township, Megantic County, Quebec, in 1831. [TNA.CO384.28.24-26; CO384.22.3-5]

MCKENZIE, CHARLES KENNETH, born 1788, died in New York on 6 July 1862. [GM.ns2/13.504]

MCKENZIE, DONALD, born 1783 in Scotland, former Governor of the Hudson Bay, Company, died in Mayville, Chataque County on 20 January 1851. [GM.ns35.454]

MCKENZIE, DUGALD, with a family of four persons, from Mid Sannox, Arran, emigrated via Lamlash, Arran, aboard the brigantine Caledonia bound for Canada in 1829, landed in Quebec on 25 June 1829. [TNA.CO384.22.3-5]

MCKENZIE, GEORGE, born 1807, in Fordyce, Banffshire, died in Halifax, Nova Scotia, on 24 November 1867. [AJ.18.12.1867]

MACKENZIE, JAMES, in Quebec, a letter to his brother Donald Mackenzie in New York, dated 1839. [NRS.16.208]

MCKENZIE, JAMES GRANT, MD, in Paragold, Arkansas, heir to his father Alexander McKenzie, a shoemaker in Aberdeen, who died on 2 July 1873, re property in Aberdeen, on 29 May 1900. [NRS.S/H]

MACKENZIE, JOHN, born 1815 in Ramshorn, Glasgow, emigrated to Kingston, Canada, in 1820. Prime Minister of Canada from 1867 until his death in 1891. [Ramshorn gravestone]

MCKENZIE, JOHN, with a family of five persons, from Sannox, Arran, bound for Canada in 1829. [TNA.CO384.22.3-5]

MCKENZIE, KENNETH JOHN, born 1799 in Stornaway, Lewis, was educated at King's College, Aberdeen from 1813 until 1820, minister of St Andrew's, Pictou, Nova Scotia, from 1823, died in 1838. [F.7.616]

MCKENZIE, KENNETH, from Skye, Inverness-shire, emigrated via Greenock aboard the Royal Adelaide bound for St John, New

Brunswick, later to Fredericton, petitioned the New Brunswick House of Assembly in 1838. [PANB.RS24/4/77]

MCKENZIE, LOUIS, born 1849 in Aberdeen, died in Ottawa, Canada West, on 15 September 1879. [AJ]

MACKENZIE, MARGARET GORDON or, born 1840, wife of William McKenzie of Kennethmont in Aberdeenshire, daughter of Charles Gordon in Peterhead, died in Mitchell, Canada West, on 8 June 1862. [AJ]

MCKENZIE or WALLACE, MARGARET, in Canada, a Deed of Factory and Commission in favour of Alexander White, dated 1 December 1864. [NRS.RD1224.45]

MCKENZIE, MARGARET, eldest daughter of William McKenzie in Ardchronie, Toronto, Ontario, married Philip Frushard Graham Bell, of Ilfracombe, Muskota, Canada, in Toronto on 25 June 1884. [S.12793]

MCKENZIE, NICOLSON COLIN, a surgeon in America, an inventory dated 1872. [NRS.SC70.158.5]

MCKENZIE, PETER, with a family of five persons, from Sannox, Arran, aboard the Caledonia bound for Canada, 1829. [TNA.CO384.22.3-5]

MCKENZIE, WILLIAM, born 1786, with a family of six persons, from Lochranza, Arran, aboard the Albion in 1829, settled in Inverness township, Megantic County, Lower Canada in 1831, died 5 April 1855, husband of Mary born 1785, died 15 March 1870. [TNA.CO384.28.24-26; CO384.22.3-5] [St Andrew's Cemetery, Inverness, Quebec]

MACKENZIE, WILLIAM LYON, born 1794 in Dundee, Angus, settled in Canada by 1825, a political radical, died in Toronto on 28 August 1861. [GM.ns2/11.567]

MCKENZIE, WILLIAM, second son of Kenneth McKenzie a builder in Gallatown, Fife, died in Attica, Indiana, on 14 February

1880, his brother David McKenzie, born 1842, died in Chicago, Illinois, on 27 December 1872. [FFP]

MCKERCHER, DONALD, settled in Reach, Ontario, by 1848, a petitioner. [NRS.GD112.61.5]

MCKERCHER, DUNCAN, settled in Reach, Ontario, by 1848, a petitioner. [NRS.GD112.61.5]

MCKERCHER, JOHN, settled in Reach, Ontario, by 1848, a petitioner. [NRS.GD112.61.5]

MCKERRALL, WILLIAM, in Dallas, Texas, an inventory dated 1874. [NRS.SC70.170.910]

MCKERROW, WILLIAM, in Arcada, Wyoming, New York, heir to his brother James McKerrow, a blacksmith in Auchenleck, Ayrshire, who died on 3 July 1888, 1 April 1889. [NRS.S/H]

ICHAN, ALEXANDER JOHN, born 31 December 1835 in Daviot, Inverness-shire, son of Reverend Dugald McKichan and his wife Isabella McPhie, was educated at the University of St Andrews from 1852 until 1856, minister at Kinlochluichart from 1869 until 1874, then at Barney's River, Nova Scotia from 1874, died in Winnipeg, Manitoba, in 1898. [StAU]

MCKICHAN, FINLAY HUGH, born 6 September 1832 in Merigovish, Nova Scotia, son of Dugald McKichan and Isabella McPhie, a student at St Andrews University in Fife, from 1851 until 1855, a schoolteacher in Melbourne, Australia, died there on 28 March 1896. [StAU]

MCKIDD, ALEXANDER, from Thurso in Caithness, was educated at King's College in Aberdeen around 1842, later a Free Church minister in Canada. [KCA]

MACKIE, ELIZABETH, in Mersea, Ontario, heir to James Mackie in Macduff, Banffshire, who died 24 May 1858. [NRS.S/H]

MACKIE, JAMES, in Ogemaw, Michigan, heir to James Mackie in Macduff, Banffshire, who died 24 May 1858. [NRS.S/H.12.8.1890]

MACKIE, JOHN, a saddler in Salem, Massachusetts, an inventory, dated 1874. [NRS.SC70.168.225]

MACKIE, or BUCHANAN, MARGARET, wife of Thomas Buchanan a goldsmith in Mersea, Ontario, heir to James Mackie in Macduff, Banffshire, who died 24 May 1858. [NRS.S/H]

MACKIE, RICHARD CONON, born 1841, son of Thomas Mackie a saddler in Aberdeen, was washed overboard from the James Yeo bound for Quebec on 22 October 1861. [AJ]

MCKILLOP, ARCHIBALD, with a family of nine persons, in Lochranza, Arran, bound for Canada, aboard the Albion in 1829. [TNA.CO384.22.3-5]

MCKILLOP, ARCHIBALD, with a family of seven persons, in Lochranza, Arran, bound via Lamlash for Quebec, aboard the Albion in 1829. [TNA.CO384.22.3-5]

MCKILLOP, Mrs CATHERINE, from Arran, with a family of five, settled in Inverness, Lower Canada, in 1831. [TNA.CO384.28.24-26]

MCKILLOP, DONALD, with a family of eight persons, in Sannox, Arran, bound via Lamlash, Arran, aboard the Caledonia, a brigantine, bound for Canada, landed at Quebec on 25 June 1829. [TNA.CO384.22.3-5]

MCKILLOP, JOHN, born 1805 in Arran, aboard the Albion to Canada in 1829, settled in Inverness, Megantic County, Lower Canada, died 4 December 1871. [Inverness gravestone, Quebec]

MCKILLOP, NEIL, with a family of eight persons, in North Sannox, Arran, bound for Canada, aboard the Caledonia, a brigantine, in 1829, landed at Quebec on 25 June 1829. [TNA.CO384.22.3-5]

MCKILLOP, PETER, with a family of nine persons, from Corrie, Arran, bound for Canada aboard the Caledonia, a brigantine, in 1829, landed in Quebec on 25 June 1829. [TNA.CO384.22.3-5]

MCKILLOP, Mrs, a widow, from Urinbeg, Arran, aboard either the Caledonia or the Albion in 1829, settled in Inverness township, Megantic County, Quebec, in 1831. [TNA.CO384.28.24-26]

MCKILLOP, Mrs, a widow, from Corrie, Arran, aboard either the Albion or the Caledonia in 1829, settled in Inverness township Megantic County, Quebec, in 1831. [TNA.CO384.28.24-26]

MCKINNISON, ARCHIBALD, born 1799, with Elizabeth McKinnison born 1813, Neil McKinnison born 1841, from North Uist, Outer Hebrides, bound via Greenock aboard the Waterhen of London to Quebec in 1849. [NRS.GD221.4435]

MCKINNON, ALEXANDER, from Corriecravie, Arran, settled in Inverness township, Megantic County, Quebec, in 1831. [TNA.CO384.28.24-26]

MCKINNON, DANIEL, from Corriecravie, Arran, settled in Inverness township, Megantic County, Quebec, in 1831. [TNA.CO384.28.24-26]

MACKINNON, JAMES, from Skye, Inverness-shire, emigrated via Greenock, Renfrewshire, aboard the Royal Adelaide bound for St John, New Brunswick, later to Fredericton, N.B., petitioned the New Brunswick House of Assembly in 1838. [PANB.RS24/4/77]

MCKINNON, JOHN, the elder, from Slidderie, Arran, settled in Inverness township, Megantic County, Quebec, in 1831. [TNA.CO384.28.24-26]

MCKINNON, JOHN, from Corriecravie, Arran, settled in Inverness township, Megantic County, Quebec, in 1831. [TNA.CO384.28.24-26]

MCKINNON, MARTIN, from Skye, Inverness-shire, emigrated via Greenock aboard the Royal Adelaide bound for St John, New Brunswick, later to Fredericton, N.B., petitioned the New Brunswick House of Assembly in 1838. [PANB.RS24/4/77]

MACKINNON, Sir WILLIAM, letters from Gerald Waller, agent of the Florida Land and Colonization Committee, dated 1877 to 1884. [NRS.NRAS.0323]

MCLACHLAN, ROBERT, in New York, heir to his father Robert McLachlan, a china merchant in Sinclairtown, Kirkcaldy, Fife, who died on 8 September 1883, on 12 December 1889. [NRS.S/H]

MCLAREN, JOHN REID, born 17 December 1848 in St Martins, Perthshire, son of William McLaren, a farmer, and his wife Charlotte Reis, was educated t St Andrews from 1868 to 1872, died in British Columbia on 7 June 1908. [SA]

MCLAREN, ROBERT GREENLAW, born 3 August 1833 in Wick, Caithness, son of James McLaren and Mary Greenlaw, was educated at the University of St Andrews, in Fife, graduated BA in 1863, minister at Three Rivers, Canada, from 1862 until 1882. [SAU]

MACLAREN, WILLIAM SCOTT, in Boston, Massachusetts, heir to his father John MacLaren an architect in Dundee, who died 20 January 1890, re property in Broughty Ferry, Angus. [NRS.S/H]

MCLEAN, ALEXANDER, from Nova Scotia, graduated MA at King's College, Aberdeen, in March 1849, later a minister at Gareloch, Nova Scotia. [KCA]

MCLEAN, ALEXANDER, born 1803, with his children Catherine born 1821, Euphemia born 1829, Neil born 1836, John born 1838, Lachlan born 1843, Rachel born 1845, Donald born 1847, and Hector born 1848, from North Uist, Outer Hebrides, emigrated via Greenock aboard the Cashmere of Glasgow bound for Quebec in 1849. [NRS.GD2214011.53]

MCLEAN, ALEXANDER, a brickmaker in Omaha, Nebraska, heir to his father Allan McLean in Dunfermline, Fife, who died on 21 July 1888, re property in Dunfermline, on 30 October 1889. [NRS.S/H]

MCLEAN, ARCHIBALD, from St Andrews, New Brunswick, a student at Marischal College in Aberdeen, in 1854. [MCA]

MCLEAN, DONALD, from Baileguish, Fhearnasdail, Glen Feshie, Inverness-shire, emigrated in 1831 to Puslinch, Upper Canada, [HS.16.4.17]

MCLEAN, DONALD, born 1799, with his wife Flora born 1807, and children Donald born 1829, John born 1832, Archibald born 1834, Lachlan born 1836, Mary born 1841, Alexander born 1845, and Ewen born 1848, from North Uist, Outer Hebrides, emigrated via Greenock aboard the Cashmere of Glasgow bound for Quebec in 1849. [NRS.GD2214011.53]

MCLEAN, DONALD, born 1820, with his wife Marion born 1824, and children Mary born 1843, and Euphemia born 1847, from North Uist, Outer Hebrides, emigrated via Greenock aboard the Cashmere of Glasgow bound for Quebec in 1849. [NRS.GD2214011.53]

MCLEAN, EWAN, in New York, an inventory dated 1877. [NRS.SC70.181.718]

MCLEAN, GEORGE, from St Andrews, New Brunswick, a student at Marischal College in Aberdeen, in 1854. [MCA]

MCLEAN, JOHN, born 1792, with Catherine McLean born 1801, Mary McLean born 1824, Margaret McLean born 1826, Neil McLean born 1829, Elizabeth McLean born 1832, Catherine McLean born 1836, from North Uist, Outer Hebrides, bound via Greenock aboard the Waterhen of London to Quebec in 1849. [NRS.GD221.4435]

MACLEAN, JOHN JENKIN, from Canada, graduated MD from Edinburgh University in 1826. [EMG]

MCLEAN, JOHN, from Nova Scotia, graduated MA from Glasgow University in 1825. [RGG]

MCLEAN, JOHN, minister of South Parish of Paisley, Renfrewshire, from 1856 until 1873, emigrated to the USA, and died there in August 1873. [F.111.183]

MCLEAN, PETER, with his wife Margaret Martin, and ten children, from Baileguish, Fhearnasdail, Glen Feshie, Inverness-shire, emigrated in 1833 to Puslinch, Upper Canada, [HS.16.4.17]

MCLEAN, Reverend PETER, born in Uig, Lewis, in 1800, was educated at King's College, Aberdeen, a schoolmaster, was sent as a missionary to Cape Breton from 1837 until 1841 a Free Church minister in Cape Breton, Nova Scotia, for five years, thereafter in Tobermory and Sandwick, died there on 28 March 1868. [Old Sandwick gravestone, Stornaway][F.7.607]

MCLEAN, WILLIAM, in Montgomery, Alabama, heir to his mother Isabella Wright or McLean or Ewing in Liverpool, England, who died on 1 March 1880, 10 May 1887. [NRS.S/H]

MACLEAY, DONALD, from Knockfarrel, Inverness, formerly a miner, emigrated via Liverpool aboard the Lake Huron in 26 March 1898 bound for Nova Scotia, landed in Halifax, N.S., on 6 April 1898. [TGSI.70.59]

MCLENNAN, JAMES, from Skye, Inverness-shire, emigrated via Greenock aboard the Royal Adelaide bound for St John, New Brunswick, later to Fredericton, N.B., petitioned the New Brunswick House of Assembly in 1838. [PANB.RS24/4/77]

MCLENNAN, JOHN, from Skye, Inverness-shire, emigrated via Greenock aboard the Royal Adelaide bound for St John, New Brunswick, later to Fredericton, N.B., petitioned the New Brunswick House of Assembly in 1838. [PANB.RS24/4/77]

MCLEOD, ALEXANDER, from Skye, Inverness-shire, emigrated via Greenock aboard the Royal Adelaide bound for St John, New Brunswick, later to Fredericton, N.B., petitioned the New Brunswick House of Assembly in 1838. [PANB.RS24/4/77]

MCLEOD, DONALD, born 1800, from Barraglom, Great Bernara, Lewis, Outer Hebrides, settled in Whitton township in 1851, died 1884. [Stornaway Pioneer Cemetery, Winslow, Quebec]

MCLEOD, DONALD, born 1793 in Luss, son of John MacLeod a farmer, was educated at Glasgow University, minister of the Presbyterian Church in Coburg, Canada, from 1851 to 1860, died in Gourock, Scotland, on 19 May 1868. [F.111.196]

MCLEOD, FLORA, daughter of Donald McLeod of Schoolhill, Aberdeen, died in Toronto on 12 June 1862. [AJ]

MCLEOD, HUGH, minister of the Free Church at Mira Ferry, Cape Breton, Nova Scotia, from 1850 until his death on 23 January 1894. [F.7.607]

MCLEOD, KENNETH, born 1811 in Lewis, Outer Hebrides, died 29 April 1891 in Quebec. [Stornaway Pioneer Cemetery, Winslow, Quebec, gravestone]

MCLEOD, MALCOLM, born 1814, with his wife Euphemia born 1814, and children Katherine born 1837, Allan born 1839, Margaret born 1843, Janet born 1846, and Alexander born 1848, from North Uist, Outer Hebrides, emigrated via Greenock aboard the Cashmere of Glasgow bound for Quebec in 1849. [NRS.GD22140l1.53]

MCLEOD, MALCOLM, born 1804, with Marion McLeod born 1814, Margaret McLeod born 1832, John McLeod born 1834, Marion McLeod born 1836, Ann McLeod born 1841, Donald McLeod born 1842, Angus McLeod born 1848, from North Uist, Outer Hebrides, bound via Greenock aboard the Waterhen of London to Quebec in 1849. [NRS.GD221.4435]

MCLEOD, MURDOCH, in Bradford, Canada, an inventory dated 1873. [NRS.SC70.164.92]

MCLEOD, RACHEL born 1811, from Barraglom, Great Bernara, Lewis, Outer Hebrides, settled in Whitton township in 1851, died 1886. [Stornaway Pioneer Cemetery, Winslow, Quebec]

MACRAE, ALEXANDER, born 1837, son of Alexander Law of Mintlaw, Aberdeenshire, died in Quebec on 18 June 1859. [AJ]

MCLEOD, RODERICK, born on Harris, was ordained minister of Strathlorne, Cape Breton, in 1886, later was minister at Kenyon and Ripley in Canada, he returned to Scotland by 1910. [F.7.607]

MCLUISH, DONALD, born 1785, with Mary McLuish born 1807, Ann McLuish born 1830, Neil McLuish born 1832, and Flora McLeish born 1834, from North Uist, Outer Hebrides, bound via Greenock aboard the Waterhen of London to Quebec in 1849. [NRS.GD221.4435]

MCLUISH, JOHN, born 1798, with his wife Kate born 1812, and children Donald born 1836, Ewan born 1838, Murdo born 1840, Mary born 1842, Donald the younger born 1844, and Christy born 1847, from North Uist, Outer Hebrides, emigrated via Greenock aboard the Cashmere of Glasgow bound for Quebec in 1849. [NRS.GD2214011.53]

MCLUISH, NORMAN, born 1802, with his wife Catherine born 1817, and children Marion born 1834, Donald born 1843, Angus born 1845, Margaret born 1847, and Archibald born 1848, from North Uist, Outer Hebrides, emigrated via Greenock aboard the Cashmere of Glasgow bound for Quebec in 1849. [NRS.GD2214011.53]MCMAY, NEIL, born 1826, with Kate McMay born 1830, from North Uist, Outer Hebrides, bound via Greenock aboard the Waterhen of London to Quebec in 1849. [NRS.GD221.4435]

MCMILLAN, DONALD, from Skye, Inverness-shire, emigrated via Greenock aboard the Royal Adelaide bound for St John, New Brunswick, later to Fredericton, N.B., petitioned the New Brunswick House of Assembly in 1838. [PANB.RS24/4/77]

MACMILLAN, JESSIE PHILIP, wife of Neil MacMillan in Victoria, Ellis County, Kansas, ultimus haeres, 28 April 1880. [NRS.PS3.17.51]

MCMILLAN, MARGARET, with a family of three persons, from South Sannox, Arran, bound via Lamlash, Arran, aboard the brigantine Caledonia for Canada, in 1829, landed at Quebec on 25 June 1829. [TNA.CO384.22.3-5]

MCMILLAN, NEIL, with a family of eight persons, from South Sannox, Arran, bound via Lamlash, Arran, aboard the brigantine Caledonia for Canada, in 1829, landed at Quebec on 25 June 1829. [TNA.CO384.22.3-5]

MCMILLAN, WILLIAM A. F., in New York, a Deed of Factory and Commission dated 1882 with his mother. [NRS.RD1865.209.182]

MACNAB, DONALD CAMPBELL, letters re a voyage to San Francisco, California, and return by rail to New York, dated 1881 to 1885. [NRS.NRAS.1126]

MACNAUGHTON, DANIEL, a farmer in Shelburn, Ontario, heir to his father Neil McNaughton, a wood turner in Glasgow, who died on 6 January 1886, 8 June 1889. [NRS.S/H]

MACNAUGHTON, JOHN, in Kaukauna, USA, was served heir to Mary and Janet Swan in Dollar, Clackmannanshire, who died on 28 April 1899 and 12 June 1898, respectively. [NRS.S/H]

MCNEILL, Major ALEXANDER, in North Carolina, a letter to his kinsman Lieutenant General Duncan Darroch of Gourock, Renfrewshire, in 1835. [NLS.Acc.9722]

MCNEILL, JOHN, in Paisley, Bruce County, Canada, an inventory dated 1873. [NRS.SC70.161.338]

MCNICOL, GRAHAM, and Company, merchants in Newfoundland, sederunt book from 1821 until 1822. [NRS.CS96.4083]

MCNISH, D., in Bermuda, a letter to Captain Archibald McDonald of the 2nd West India Regiment in Jamaica, dated 28 February 1807. [NRS.GD47.754]

MCPHAIL, ARCHIBALD, born 1823, with Christian McPhail born 1824, Christian McPhail born 1848, from North Uist, Outer Hebrides, bound via Greenock aboard the Waterhen of London to Quebec in 1849. [NRS.GD221.4435]

MCPHAIL, JAMES, born 1785, a shoemaker from Strichen, Aberdeenshire, died in Hamilton, Ontario, in 1877. [AJ]

MCPHAIL, JOHN, born 1780, from Strichen, Aberdeenshire, died in Nichol, Canada West, on 31 October 1867. [AJ]

MCPHERSON, CHARLES, from Skye, emigrated via Greenock aboard the Royal Adelaide bound for St John, New Brunswick, later to Fredericton, N.B., petitioned the New Brunswick House of Assembly in 1838. [PANB.RS24/4/77]

MCPHERSON, DONALD, born 1796, with Catherine McPherson born 1827, Flora McPherson born 1831, Donald McPherson born 1835, Lauchlan McPherson born 1837, Angus McPherson born 1840, from North Uist, Outer Hebrides, bound via Greenock aboard the Waterhen of London to Quebec in 1849. [NRS.GD221.4435]

MCPHERSON, FREDERICK ANGUS, a farmer in Kalamazoo, Michigan, heir to his father Donald McPherson there, who died on 20 June 1887, re property in Kirriemuir, Angus, on 1 November 1889. [NRS.S/H]

MCPHERSON, JOHN, in Boston, USA, an inventory dated in 1873. [NRS.SC70.163.117]

MACPHERSON, JONATHAN, born 1862, from Nairnside, in Inverness, formerly a blacksmith, emigrated via Liverpool aboard the Lake Huron in 26 March 1898 bound for Nova Scotia, landed in Halifax, N.S., on 6 April 1898, from there to the Yukon. [TGSI.70.59]

MCPHERSON, NEIL, born 1799, his wife Kate born 1814, and children Archibald born 1833, John born 1835, Margaret born 1839, James born 1842, Flora born 1844, and Alexander born 1846, from

North Uist, Outer Hebrides, emigrated via Greenock aboard the Cashmere of Glasgow bound for Quebec in 1849. [NRS.GD2214011.53]

MCPHERSON, NEIL, from Skye, Inverness-shire, emigrated via Greenock aboard the Royal Adelaide bound for St John, New Brunswick, later to Fredericton, N.B., petitioned the New Brunswick House of Assembly in 1838. [PANB.RS24/4/77]

MACPHIE, DONALD, from Skye, Inverness-shire, emigrated via Greenock aboard the Royal Adelaide bound for St John, New Brunswick, later to Fredericton, N.B., petitioned the New Brunswick House of Assembly in 1838. [PANB.RS24/4/77]

MACRAE, ALEXANDER, born 1829, a blacksmith from Fort Augustus, Inverness-shire, emigrants aboard the Annie Jane of Liverpool, master William Mason, bound from Liverpool to Quebec, was shipwrecked and drowned near Vatersay in the Outer Hebrides on 28 September 1853. [WAJ]

MACRAE, RODERICK C., born at Pinette, Prince Edward Island, in 1857, son of Captain Donald MacRae, graduated MA from Glasgow University in 1880. [RGG]

MCRAE, DONALD, from Skye, Inverness-shire, emigrated via Greenock aboard the Royal Adelaide bound for St John, New Brunswick, later to Fredericton, N.B., petitioned the New Brunswick House of Assembly in 1838. [PANB.RS24/4/77]

MACRITCHIE, THOMAS ELDER, in Kansas, an inventory, dated 1876. [NRS.SC70.176.469]

MCRONALD, ALEXANDER, in Toronto, Ontario, heir to his brother Thomas McRonald a mason, son of Thomas McRonald a wright in Maybole, Ayrshire, who died on 20 August 1870. [NRS.S/H]

MACTAGGART, JOHN, formerly a Civil Engineer on the Rideau Canal in Canada, an author, died in Tors, Kirkcudbright, on 8 January 1830. [GM.100.285]

MACTAVISH, GEORGINA, daughter of the late J. G. MacTavish in Montreal, Quebec, married N. W. Massey, son of George Massey, in Pitlochry, Perthshire, on 21 October 1863. [GM.ns2/15.773]

MCTAVISH, HUGH GEORGE, in Virginia, an inventory dated 1873. [NRS.SC70.165.178]

MACTAVISH, JOHN, born 1787, British Consul in Maryland, died in Baltimore, Maryland, on 21 June 1852. [GM.ns38.213]

MCVITTIE, DAVID, on Prince Edward Island, a sasine dated 3 February 1900. [NRS.R.S.Lochmaben, Dumfries-shire,11.288]

MCVITTIE or GILPIN, SARAH, of 233 Liberty Street, Paterson, New Jersey, a sasine dated 16 July 1900. [NRS.R.S.Lochmaben, Dumfries-shire, 12.13]

MAIR, THOMAS, born 1786, from Ellon, Aberdeenshire, died in Bellfield, Elora, Canada West on 29 March 1862. [AJ]

MAIR, WILLIAM, son of James Mair a schoolteacher in New Deer in Aberdeenshire, graduated MA from Marischal College, Aberdeen, in 1846, a Church of Scotland minister in Canada. [MCA]

MAIR, Mrs THOMAS, born 1795, from Aberdeenshire, settled in Nichol, Canada West, in 1835, died there on7 November 1874. [AJ]

MAITLAND, STUART, in New York, a marriage certificate with Margaret S. Lynch, dated 12 November 1841. [NRS.RD1180.771]

MALCOLM, FRANCIS, born 1792, a farmer from Aberdeenshire, died in Zorra, Canada West, on 29 September 1866. [AJ]

MALCOLM. THOMAS, from Boathole, Durris, Kincardineshire, died in Hamilton, Upper Canada on16 September1853, and his wife Ann Nicol, died on 16 September 1853. [AJ]

MALLOCH, EDWARD, in Ottawa, Canada, an inventory dated 1872. [NRS.SC70.157.497].

MANSON, GEORGE, father of a daughter born at Roseburn, Birdtail Creek, Manitoba, on 10 September 1884, [S.12867]; at Shoal Lake, Manitoba, was served heir to his father Andrew Manson in Wick, Caithness, who died on 7 June 1893. [NRS.S/H]

MANSON, WILLIAM, in Vancouver, British Columbia, was served heir to his uncle Andrew Manson in Wick, Caithness, who died on 7 June 1893. [NRS.S/H]

MANTACH, ROBERT, from Rothes in Moray, graduated BD from King's College in Aberdeen on 27 September 1840, a minister of the Church of England in Bermuda. [KCA]

MARSHALL, ROBERT, in Ocala, East Florida, a sasine dated 19 March 1888. [NRS.R.S.Whithorn. 6.214]

MARSHALL, WALTER, in Chicago, Illinois, heir to his father Walter Marshall, a spirit dealer in Alloa, Clackmannanshire, who died on 23 August 1866, re property in Alloa, on 24 November 1887. [NRS.S/H]

MARTIN, ANN EDWARDS, second daughter of Alexander Martin a compositor in Edinburgh, died in New York on 9 June 1884. [S.12789]

MARTIN, DONALD, from Soillerie, Fhearnasdail, Glen Feshie, Inverness-shire, emigrated in 1831 to Puslinch, Upper Canada, [HS.16.4.17]

MARTIN, JAMES, MD, surgeon in the Royal Navy, in Halifax, Nova Scotia, an inventory dated 1873. [NRS.SC70.162.570]

MARTIN, JOHN DOUGLAS, in Chicago, Illinois, eldest son of John S. Martin of the Bank of Scotland in Edinburgh, married Ada Balance Allen from Pembrokeshire, Wales, in Minneapolis, Minnesota, on 20 April 1885. [S.13061]

MARTIN, JOHN, a blacksmith, son of John Martin in Burntisland, Fife, died in Ansonia, Connecticut, on 15 January 1899. [S.17353]

MARTIN, JOHN, a travelling agent of 252, 54th Street, Brooklyn, New York, a sasine dated 12 December 1899. [NRS.R.S.Lochmaben, Dumfries-shire,11.279]

MARTIN, JOHN WRIGHT, in Brooklyn, New York, was served heir to his aunt Anne Wright, widow of John Wright a master mariner in Lochmaben, Dumfries-shire, who died on 22 July 1899. [NRS.S/H]

MARWICK, HUGH, from Rendall in Orkney, in Hudson Bay Company Service in 1805. [OA]

MATHIE, HUGH, a merchant in Glasgow, trading with Nassau, New Providence, Quebec, Baltimore, Virginia, Montreal, the West Indies, and Martinique around 1803. [NRS.CS96.3231]

MATHESON, JOHN, from Skye, Inverness-shire, emigrated via Greenock aboard the Royal Adelaide bound for St John, New Brunswick, later to Fredericton, N.B., petitioned the New Brunswick House of Assembly in 1838. [PANB.RS24/4/77]

MATHESON, ROBERT POPE, in Dutil, New Mexico, was served heir to his father William James Matheson in Edinburgh, who died on 17 June 1892, and to his grandfather Robert Matheson of West Coates, an architect in Edinburgh, who died on 5 March 1877. [NRS.S/H]

MATHESON, RORY, from Skye, Inverness-shire, emigrated via Greenock aboard the Royal Adelaide bound for St John, New Brunswick, later to Fredericton, N.B., petitioned the New Brunswick House of Assembly in 1838. [PANB.RS24/4/77]

MATHIESON, ANGUS, a blacksmith from Dornoch in Easter Ross, an emigrant aboard the Annie Jane of Liverpool, master William Mason, bound from Liverpool to Quebec, was shipwrecked but survived near Vatersay in the Outer Hebrides on 28 September 1853. [WAJ]

MEIKLE, GEORGE, a carpenter in Galston, Pennsylvania, heir to his brother William Meikle, gas manager in Longford, Ireland, who died on 10 October 1876, 15 February 1900. [NRS.S/H]

MEIKLEHAM, DAVID SCOTT, MD, born 1805 in Glasgow, son of Professor Meikleham, died in New York on 20 November 1849. [GM.ns.33.342]

MELLISS, DAVID ERNEST, a civil and mining engineer in San Francisco, California, heir to his grand-aunt Agnes McHattie, widow of Reverend Professor Michael Willis in Toronto, Ontario, who died 24 February 1890, re property in Glasgow. [NRS.S/H.25.10.1890]

MENTEATH, THOMAS LOUGHNAN STUART, a Captain of the US Army, formerly of the 16th Lancers, second son of the late Sir Charles Granville Stuart Menteath, died in Canandaqua, Ontario, on 22 February 1854. [GM.ns41.554]; in Canandaignia, New York, an inventory dated 1872. [NRS.SC70.159.982]

MENZIES, WILLIAM BRADFORD HARDING, a merchant in Old Fort, North Carolina, heir to his father William Menzies jr there who died 28 April 1890. [NRS.S/H]

MEUDELL, GEORGE HERCHIMER, in Arcadis, South California, was served heir to his uncle William Meudell [son of William Fabian Meudell in Brockville, Upper Canada] who died on 7 December 1868, also to his aunt Helen Meudell [daughter of said William Fabian Meudell] who died on 4 July 1886; and to his father George Meudell, a mercantile agent in Chicago, Illinois, 'who died between 20 and 30 years ago. [NRS.S/H]

MEWHORT, LOUISE, in Montreal, Canada, was served heir to his mother Jane Ann Malloch, wife of Wilson Mewhort in St Anne's, Montreal, who died 18 May 1898, re property in South Street, Perth. [NRS.S/H]

MIDDLETON, WILLIAM ABERDEIN, in Anniston, Alabama, heir to his father William Middleton, a bleacher in Downfield, Dundee, who died on 10 May 1886, re property in Brechin, Angus, on 26 October 1900. [NRS.S/H]

MILES, THOMAS, born 1832, son of Thomas Miles and his wife Margaret Thomson, drowned at North Fork on the American River, California, on 24 May 1852. [St Andrews Cathedral gravestone, Fife]

MILLER, ALEXANDER, son of James Miller in St Andrews, Fife, died in Montreal, Quebec, on 24 February 1850. [FH]

MILLER, DAVID, in Cleveland, Ohio, a sasine dated 23 September 1889. [NRS.R.S.Forfar, Angus, 48.137]

MILLER, JAMES, late merchant in New Providence in the Bahamas, now in Edinburgh, versus Elisabeth Fowler, spouse of Dr Mitchell in Virginia, 1815. [NRS.GD63.478]

MILLER, JAMES, born 1816, died at 22 West 48th Street, New York, on 10 September 1884. [S.12847]

MILLER, JAMES, in Kingswood, West Virginia, heir to his granduncle John Miller, a feuar in Crosstone, Motherwell, Lanarkshire, who died 10 July 1882, 8 June 1889. [NRS.S/H]

MILLAR, JOHN, from Dalton, Dumfriesshire, with seven children, emigrated to Canada in 1834 settled in Edwardsburgh, Grenville County, Ontario. [LAC.MG24.I67]

MILLAR, MARGARET, born 1846, wife of Robert Stein from Edinburgh, died in Pittston, Luzerne County, Pennsylvania, in 1884. [S.12877]

MILLAR, THOMAS, a farm servant in Londesborough, Huron, Ontario, heir to his sister Jean Millar in Drayton, Wellington, Ontario, who died on 20 May 1880. [NRS.S/H]

MILLER, WILLIAM, in Marrasonack, USA, an inventory dated 1871. [NRS.SC70.153.298]

MILLER, FERGUS, and Company, merchants in Newfoundland, sederunt book from 1820 until 1823. [NRS.CS16.3618]

MITCHELL, ANNE, wife of John Johnston in Knoxville, Illinois, was granted the lands of Rufflatts on 20 December 1842. [RGS.228.25]

MITCHELL, JOHN, a merchant in Glasgow, trading with Jamaica, Demerara, Trinidad, New York, Nova Scotia, and Quebec, in 1818. [NRS.CS96.3457]

MITCHELL, JOHN, a shipmaster in St John's, Newfoundland, an inventory dated 1878. [NRS.SC70.192.149]

MITCHELL, PETER, in New York, a deed dated 16 September 1831. [NRS.RD445.684]

MITCHELL, THOMAS, son of Robert Mitchell and his wife Margaret Carmichael, died in Montreal, Quebec, on 10 August 1848. [St Andrews Cathedral gravestone, in Fife]

MITCHELL, WILLIAM, in Virginia, power of attorney in favour of William Irvine dated 18 April 1826. [NRS.RD417.499]

MONDEL, JOHN, born 1797, with Kate Mondel born 1829, Mary Mondel born 1831, John Mondel born 1837, from North Uist, Outer Hebrides, bound via Greenock aboard the Waterhen of London to Quebec in 1849. [NRS.GD221.4435]

MONTGOMERY, DONALD, son of Hugo Montgomery a merchant in New Brunswick, graduated MA from Marischal College in Aberdeen in 1843, a schoolmaster in Dollar, Clackmannanshire. [MCA]

MORE, ARTHUR WILLIAM, born 1865, son of Robert More, a merchant, and his wife Jessie Berwick, died in Victoria, British Columbia, on 17 February 1908. [St Andrews Cathedral gravestone, Fife]

MORGAN, ELIZA B., in Placentia, Newfoundland, letters to Miss Stewart dated from 1893 and 1895. [NRS.GD38.2.89/9-11]

MORRIS, FREDERICK WILLIAM, from Nova Scotia, graduated MD from Edinburgh University in 1825. [EMG]

MORRIS, WILLIAM GARDINER, MD, born 1826, son of J. Pemberton Morris in Bolton, Pennsylvania, and grandson of Reverend Dr Gardiner in Edinburgh, died in Delhi, India, on 13 January 1858. [CM.21368]

MORRISON, DAVID W., father of a daughter who was born at Rat Portage, Canada, on 19 February 1885. [S.12817]

MORRISON, DONALD, born 1789, with his wife Fiona born 1804, and children Mary born 1828, Donald born 1832, Jane born 1836, Kenneth born 1839, Catherine born 1841, and Christy born 1844, from North Uist, Outer Hebrides, emigrated via Greenock aboard the Cashmere of Glasgow to Quebec in 1849. [NRS.GD22140 11.53]

MORISON, or TODD, ELIZABETH, in Austin, Minnesota, heir to her father Joseph Morison in Glasgow who died on 15 February 1889. [NRS.S/H]

MORRISON, JAMES, minister at Dartmouth, Halifax Harbour, Nova Scotia, in 1829, at Laurencetown in 1833, and Warwick, Bermuda, in 1839. [F.7.617]

MORRISON, JOHN, son of Mark Morrison, late of Slelmorlie and Edinburgh, brother of R. Morrison, postmaster in Tranent, died in Chicago, Illinois, on 27 January 1899. [S.17348]

MORRISON, Mrs M., in Virginia, Power of Attorney in favour of F. Higgins dated 4 September 1829. [NRS.RD414.377]

MORISON, Dr RODERICK, settled in Bridgeport, Mississippi, a letter to his cousin Mrs Annabella Mackenzie in Dunvegan, Skye, Inverness-shire, on 20 March 1840. [NRS.GD403.68.7]

MOUNSEY, ALEXANDER, from Dumfries-shire, then in Vaughan township, York County, Upper Canada, a petition, 1861. [NLS.ms193]

MUNDELL, EDWARD, from Ruthwell, Dumfries-shire, settled in Edwardsburgh, Ontario, in 1830s. [LAC.MG24.I67, File 1]

MUNN, ARCHIBALD, in Newfoundland, an inventory dated 1877. [NRS.SC70.186.695]

MUNN, JAMES, born 1784, emigrated from Argyll to Prince Edward Island in 1812, died in Pictou, Nova Scotia, in 1833. [Woods Islands Pioneer Cemetery, PEI]

MUNN, JOHN, a merchant in Harbour Grace, Newfoundland, and the log-book of the brig William Punton dating from 1853 to 1854. [NRS.CS96.4477]

MUNN, ROBERT S., a merchant who emigrated to Newfoundland in 1851, settled on the Avalon Peninsula. [MU]

MUNRO, FREDERICK, a pattern-maker, in 1491 Chicago Avenue, Chicago, Illinois, a sasine dated 2 April 1908. [NRS.RS.Forfar, Angus, 73/6]

MUNRO, HUGH, a rail contractor and builder from Loan of Tulloch, with Margaret MacCulloch of Munro from Balnagowan, and female infant Munro, emigrants aboard the Annie Jane of Liverpool, master William Mason, bound from Liverpool to Quebec, was shipwrecked and drowned near Vatersay in the Outer Hebrides on 28 September 1853. [WAJ]

MURCHIE, DONALD, from Arran, settled in Inverness township, Quebec, in 1831. [TNA.CO.384.28.24/26]

MURCHIE, WILLIAM, from Ballymichail, Arran, settled in Inverness township, Megantic County, Quebec, in 1831. [TNA.CO384.28.24-26]

MURDOCH. CHARLES, with a family of nine, a shoemaker in Glen, Arran, bound for Canada, 1829. [TNA.CO384.22.3-5]

MURDOCH, JOHN LOGAN, of Nova Scotia, graduated MA from Glasgow University in 1825. [RGG]

MURRAY, JAMES, MA, an alumni, minister of St George's, Bermuda, graduated DD at King's College, Aberdeen, in September 1841. [KCA]

MURRAY, JAMES, son of Patrick Murray a writer [lawyer] in Glasgow, died at Taylor's Mount, Baltimore County, Maryland, on 4 June 1885. [S.13090]

MURRAY, JAMES, father of a son born in Sunnyside, St John's, Newfoundland, on 14 March 1885. [S.13006]

MURRAY, ROBERT, in Canada, appointed H. Dickson as his commission agent on 8 December 1831. [NRS.RD458.330.69]

MURRAY, ROBERT, a joiner, an emigrant aboard the Annie Jane of Liverpool, master William Mason, bound from Liverpool to Quebec, was shipwrecked and drowned near Vatersay in the Outer Hebrides on 28 September 1853. [WAJ]

MURRAY, WILLIAM, manager of the Bank of British Columbia, father of a son born in Vancouver, British Columbia, on 24 January 1898. [S.17035]

MUSHET, JOHN MACFARLANE, son of William Mushet in Dalkeith, Midlothian, died in Lexington, Kentucky, on 1 December 1884. [S.12919]

NAY, JOHN, in St Catherine's, Canada, an inventory dated 1875. [NRS.SC70.176.341]

NEILSEN, CARL, in Harshaw, Arizona, heir to his mother Janet Wright, wife of Carl Neilsen a ship-broker in Dundee, Angus, who died in February 1863. [NRS.S/H]; also, to her brother William Neilson [sic] a writer in Glasgow, who died on 16 May 1884. [NRS.S/H]

NEILSON, CATHERINE, born 1799, with Allan McKenzie born 1826, from North Uist, Outer Hebrides, bound via Greenock aboard the Waterhen of London to Quebec in 1849. [NRS.GD221.4435]

NESS, FLORENCE, second daughter of Alexander Ness of 3 Bernard Terrace, Edinburgh, married Reverend Joseph Elliot, Vankleet Hill, Ontario, in Montreal, Quebec, on 17 June 1884. [S.12796]

NICOL, ALEXANDER, born 1823, third son of John Nicol a builder in Lauriston, Edinburgh, died in Kingston, North Carolina, on 6 October 1884. [S.12920]

NICOL, DANIEL, from West Bennan, Arran, settled in Inverness township, Megantic County, Quebec, in 1831. [TNA.CO384.28.24-26]

NIDDRIE, WILLIAM, in Guelph, Canada, an inventory dated 1878. [NRS.SC70.187.958]

NISBET, GEORGE, father of a son born at Jermyn Farm, Minnedosa, Manitoba, on 2 January 1899. [S.17341]

NORRIE, DAVID, born 1837, late of the Royal High School in Edinburgh, died in 682 Osgood Street, Chicago, Illinois, on 9 January 1899. [S.17343]

NORIE, JAMES, in Truro, Nova Scotia, four letters to George Duncan in Elgin, Moray, from 1833 to 1842. [AUL.mss3015]

OLIPHANT, WILLIAM, born 1844, son of Walter Oliphant a publisher in Edinburgh, died in Clifford, Ontario, in 1885. [S.13038]

OMAN, EDWARD, from Clouston in Orkney, later of the Hudson Bay Company in 1845. [OA]

O'REILLY, THOMAS, in Philadelphia, Pennsylvania, heir to his father Michael Reilly, a police officer in Edinburgh, who died on 2 November 1884, re property there, 21 February 1900. [NRS.S/H]

ORD, JOHN, an architect, father of a son born at 3201 Powelton Avenue, Philadelphia, Pennsylvania, on 19 October 1884. [S.12889]

ORMOND, HELEN, daughter of the late James Ormond in Leith, Midlothian, died in Florida on 27 August 1841. [GM.ns.17.118]

ORR, ANN, in New York, heir to her father John Orr in Sherbrook, Canada, who died on 4 August1874, re property in Dunfermline, Fife, on 13 October 1887. [NRS.S/H]

ORMOND, JAMES, in Atlanta, Georgia, a deed in favour of Robert Christie, dated 2 August 1865. [NRS.RD1250.598]OVENS, HUGH, in Somerset, Nebraska, was served heir to his mother Eleanor Kennedy Crawford, wife of Thomas Ovens in Setonfield, Cockenzie, East Lothian, who died on 18 November 1895, re property at Bridge of Earn, Perthshire. [NRS.S/H]

PARKER, GEORGE, a merchant in Hamilton, Canada, an inventory dated 1876. [NRS.SC70.177.754]

PATERSON, JOHN ANDREW, a barrister in Toronto, Ontario, was served heir to his mother Jean Balfour Allison or Paterson there, who died on 16 February 1889. [NRS.S/H]

PATTERSON, ROBERT S., from Nova Scotia, graduated MA from Glasgow University in 1825. [RGG]

PATTISON, JAMES, a joiner late of 19 Caledonian Crescent, Edinburgh, father of a son born at 29 Garden Street, Hoboken, New Jersey, on 19 November 1884. [S.12919]

PATTISON, WILLIAM, a salesman in Norwich, Connecticut, heir to his uncle Joseph Pattison in Kelso, Roxburghshire, who died on 28 February 1888, re property in Kelso, on 1 February 1889. [NRS.S/H]

PAUL, THOMAS FARQUHAR, in Crescent City, Florida, heir to his father Alexander Paul, a manufacturer in Glasgow, who died on 19 November 1890, re property in Glasgow, on 10 April 1900. [NRS.S/H]

PEAT, ISABELL, in Pickering, Canada West, letters to the Mitchell family in Cupar, Fife, letters from 1835 until 1842. [AUL.ms37515]

PEAT, WILLIAM, in USA, trustees, a deed dated 25 April 1865. [NRS.RD1237.182]

PETER, JOHN, in Bruneau Valley, Idaho, heir to his cousin Arabella Peter in Ferry-port-on-Craig, Fife, who died on 9 December 1897. [NRS.S/H]

PHILIP, DAVID, in Hamilton, Canada West, ultimus haeres, on 28 April 1880. [NRS.PS3.17.51]

PHILIP, JESSIE, wife of Neil McMillan in Victoria, Ellis County, Kansas, ultimus haeres, on 28 April 1880. [NRS.PS3.17.51]

PICKMORE, Admiral, Governor of Newfoundland, letters from 1817 until 1818. [NRS.GD45.3.25]

PINKERTON, ALLAN, born 1819 in Glasgow, a cooper who emigrated to Dundee near Chicago, Illinois, in 1842, founder of the Pinkerton National Detective Agency, died in 1884.

PIRIE, JOHN, born 1860 son of James Pirie farmer in Auchmaleddie [1821-1904] and his wife Margaret Milne [1825-1909], died in Moscow, Pennsylvania, on 2 July 1904. [New Deer gravestone, Aberdeenshire]

PITTS, JAMES, of Nova Scotia, graduated MB from Glasgow University in 1869. [RGG]

PLAYFAIR, HUGH LYON, fourth son of Patrick Playfair of Ardmillan, died in Los Angeles, California, on 21 May 1885. [S.13063]

PONTON, GRACE, and spouse in Canada, granted W. H. Ponton Power of Attorney on 29 March 1832. [NRS.RD468.749.]

POTTER, JAMES, in Kansas, an inventory dated 1876. [NRS.SC70.180.480]

POTTER, Mrs M. A. POLLOCK or, in Fredericksburg, [Virginia?], an inventory dated 1876. [NRS.SC70.179.472]

PRIMROSE, FRANCIS NEIL, born 1832, eldest son of Francis Ward Primrose, died in Quebec on 24 November 1864. [GM.ns.2.18.119]

PRIMROSE, FRANCIS W., brother of the Earl of Roseberry, died in Quebec on 26 May 1860. [GM.ns.2.9.211]

PRIMROSE, JOHN WILSON, in South Minneapolis, Minnesota, heir to his aunt Sarah Primrose in Edinburgh who died between 1838 and 1843, on 8 June 1887. [NRS.S/H]

PRINGLE, BEATRIX, in Canada, a probative letter in favour of William Duncan, dated 17 April 1830, [NRS.RD414.55]

PROCTOR, JAMES H., father of a son born in Southesk farm, Elkhorn, Manitoba, on 7 October 1884. [S.12885]

PURDIE, STEPHEN ANDERSON, second son of Reverend Joseph Purdie in Clyde Vale, Crossford, Lanarkshire, died in Frederick, New Brunswick, on 1 January 1898. [S.17018]

PURVES, JOHN HOME, born 1785, eldest son of Sir Alexander Purves of Purves Hall, Berwickshire, Her Majesty's Consul in Pensacola, Florida, died there on 30 September 1827. [GM.97.573]

PURVIS, JOHN, in Mississippi, executors, Power of Attorney in favour of J. and R. MacAndrew, dated 17 December 1864. [NRS.RD1226.359]

PURVES, JOHN ARCHIBALD, in Toronto, Canada, an inventory dated 1877. [NRS.SC70.183.71]

PYE, JOHN, in St John's, Newfoundland, a sasine dated 1 May 1899. [NRS.R.S.Dysart, Fife, 7.7]

RAE, GEORGE MACAULEY, in New York, an inventory dated 1878. [NRS.SC70.190.534]

RAITT, JAMES, in Manchester, New Hampshire, heir to his father Alexander Raitt in Arbroath, Angus, who died on 6 April 1868, on 30 May 1900. [NRS.S/H]

RAMSAY, Lieutenant General GEORGE, Lord Dalhousie, was appointed Commander in Chief of HM Forces in Upper and Lower Canada, New Brunswick, Nova Scotia, Prince Edward Island, Cape Breton, Newfoundland and Bermuda on 21 October 1819. [NRS.GD45.15.104]

RANKEN, WILLIAM, born 1813, son of William Ranken a squarewright [architect] in Fraserburgh, Aberdeenshire, died in New York on 21 June 1853. [Fraserburgh Kirkton gravestone]

RANNIE, WILLIAM ROSS, a merchant in Pen Yan, New York, heir to his aunt Alexina Rannie in Turriff, Aberdeenshire, who died on 19 June 1875, on 26 March 1889. [NRS.S/H]

RANNY, MALCOLM, of New Brunswick, graduated MD from Glasgow University in 1855. [RGG]

RATE, JOHN E., born 1864, younger son of George Rate at Mungo's Wells, East Lothian, died in Portland, Oregon, on 26 May 1885. [S.13081]

RATTRAY, DAVID, from Helensburgh, Dunbartonshire, died in Hamilton, Canada West, on 5 September 1859. [GM.ns.2.7.541].

RAY, Mrs MARGARET, was born in Scotland in 1776, died in Fayetteville District, North Carolina, in October 1849. [FMS/NC]

REDMAN, JAMES, in Seattle, Washington, letters re the Washington Ironworks there, from 1894 to 1895. [NRS.NRAS.219]

REED, Reverend, born in Scotland, died in Erie County, Pennsylvania, in 1858. [GM.ns.20.428]

REEKIE, ISABELLA, daughter of Reverend David Ross in Burntisland, Fife, wife of J. R. Reekie in Quebec, died in Burntisland on 3 July 1859. [GM.ns.2.9.199]

REID, Dr DAVID BOSWELL, born in Edinburgh, grandson of Hugh Arnot, died in Washington, D.C. on 5 April 1863. [GM.ns2.14.803]

REID, FRANCES BALFOUR, second daughter of Captain James Murray Reid of the Hudson Bay Company, married William John MacDonald, at Fort Victoria, Vancouver Island, on 17 March 1857. [GM.ns.2.3.212]

REID, FRANCIS CHALMERS, in Fergus, Canada, an inventory, dated 1877. [NRS.SC70.183.824]

REID, HELEN, born 1810, daughter of John Reid, an advocate, also widow of William Weir, an advocate, died in Brantford, Canada, on 6 September 1884. [S.12880]

REID, JAMES, in Lennoxville, Canada East, married Mary Jane Reid, only child of Thomas Reid, Major of the 33rd Regiment, in Edinburgh, on 19 April 1865. [GM.ns.2/18.779]

REID, MARY ANDERSON or, in Canada, an inventory dated 1871. [NRS.SC70.155.418]

REID, ROBERT, in New London, Connecticut, an inventory dated 1876. [NRS.SC70.181.90]

RENNIE, ADAM, in Grahamston, trading with Newfoundland and Quebec from 1801 until 1807. [NRS.CS96.1306]

RICHARDSON, DAVID, in Denver, Colorado, a sasine dated 28 April 1890. [NRS.R.S.Lochmaben, Dumfries-shire, 10.105].

RICHARDSON, Mrs LOUISA WILHELMINA or GEMMILL, in Quebec, an inventory dated 1878. [NRS.SC70.190.748]

RICHMOND, THOMAS, in Ontario, an inventory dated 1877. [NRS.SC70.184.256]. [NRS.S/H]

RIDDELL, ANDREW, in Rosebank, Manitoba, was served heir to his father Thomas Riddell, a farmer in Hundalee, Jedburgh, Roxburghshire, who died on 27 April 1892. [NRS.S/H]

RITCHIE, ALEXANDER DALRYMPLE, in Seward, Nebraska, heir to his mother Jane Thomson or Veitch or Ritchie in Edinburgh, who died on 9 November 1847, on 9 May 1887. [NRS.S/H]

RITCHIE, JAMES, a commission agent in New York, an inventory dated 1873. [NRS.SC70.162.492]

RITCHIE, JAMES MEIN, in British Columbia, an inventory, dated 1879. [NRS.SC70.193.888]

RITCHIE, JOHN, an engineer in Montreal, Quebec, heir to his father John Ritchie a farmer in Blackness, who died on 21 July 1858, on 14 August 1889. [NRS.SH]

ROBERTS, JAMES, born 1840, from Forfar, Angus, died at 175 West 45th Street, New York, on 18 March 1885. [S.13017]

ROBERTSON, ANGUS, from Urinbeg, Arran, settled in Inverness township, Megantic County, Quebec, in 1831. [TNA.CO384.28.24-26]

ROBERTSON, DANIEL T., an attorney and counsellor at law in New York, was served heir to his father Daniel Robertson, a brass founder there, who died on 9 April 1877, re property in Portobello, Edinburgh. [NRS.S/H]

ROBERTSON, FREDERICK W., in USA, a Deed of Power of Attorney in favour of John Wright, dated 31 January 1865. [NRS.1231.122]

ROBERTSON, GEORGE I., in Illinois, Power of Attorney in favour of A. H. Turnbull dated 31 December 1864. [NRS.RD1226.454]

ROBERTSON, JAMES, a farmer in Still Water Village, Easter County of Washington, a letter dated 1830. [NRS.GD16.35.48]

ROBERTSON, JOHN, from Kilpatrick, Arran, settled in Inverness township, Megantic County, Quebec, in 1831. [TNA.CO384.28.24-26]

ROBERTSON, JOHN, in Philadelphia, Pennsylvania, appointed R. S. Cummings as his commission agent on 19 June 1832. [NRS.RD467.125.145]

ROBERTSON, JOHN MURDOCH, born 1854, from Edinburgh, died in New York on 5 June 1885. [S.13077]

ROBERTSON, JOHN STUART, born 1855, son of Dr Joseph Robertson of HM Register House in Edinburgh, died in Louisville, Kentucky, on 31 October 1884. [S.12906]

ROBERTSON, SARA, daughter of James Robertson in Prestonpans, Midlothian, married Peter Milne, at 593 Ontario Street, Montreal, Quebec, on 23 January 1885. [S.12977]

ROBERTSON, THOMAS, in the township of Ops, Canada, an inventory dated 1879. [NRS.SC70.194.1008]

ROBERTSON, WILLIAM, in Yorkville, Wisconsin, an inventory dated 1876. [NRS.SC70.177.1078]

RODGERS, CHARLES WILLIAM, born in County Clare, residing in Kilbirnie, Ayrshire, emigrant aboard the Annie Jane of Liverpool, master William Mason, bound from Liverpool to Quebec, was shipwrecked and drowned near Vatersay in the Outer Hebrides on 28 September 1853. [WAJ]

RODGERS, ELIZABETH, eldest daughter of Alexander Rodgers a stationer in Montrose, Angus, died at 49 Bonner Avenue, New Jersey, on 20 January 1899. [S.17351]

RODGERS, TIMOTHY, born 1815 in County Clare, residing in Kilburnie, Ayrshire, with John Rodgers born 1837 and James Rodgers born 1840, emigrants aboard the Annie Jane of Liverpool, master William Mason, bound from Liverpool to Quebec, was shipwrecked but survived near Vatersay in the Outer Hebrides on 28 September 1853. [WAJ]

ROGERSON, JAMES, in St John's, Newfoundland, to Samuel Rogerson in Leithenhall by Moffat, dated 16 May 1861. [NRS.GD1.620.94]

ROGERSON, ROBERT, MD, on Staten Island, New York, heir to his father George Rogerson of Pearsbyhall, who died on 12 August 1886, re lands in Lochmaben, Dumfries-shire, on 4 October 1887. [NRS.S/H]

ROGERSON, SAMUEL, in St John's, Newfoundland, a letter to his brother William Rogerson at Hutton, near Lockerbie, Dumfries-shire, dated 18 November 1820; another to brother David Rogerson in Leithenhall by Moffat, Dumfriesshire, dated 26 November 1820. [NRS.GD1.620.66/67]

RONALDSON, THOMAS, in Lorin, California, heir to his mother Margaret Stobie, wife of William Ronaldson a farmer in Balneathil, who died on 16 November 1888, re lands in Portmoak, Kinross-shire, on 3 September 1889. [NRS.S/H]

ROSE, CHARLES, born 1793 in Nairn, Moray, formerly a Lieutenant of the Royal Navy, residing in Melbourne East, Quebec, with his wife Miriam Rose, born 1797 in Devonport, England, emigrants aboard the Annie Jane of Liverpool, master William Mason, bound from Liverpool to Quebec, was shipwrecked and drowned near Vatersay in the Outer Hebrides on 28 September 1853. [WAJ]

ROSS, ALEXANDER, born 1828, an engineer from the Gorbals in Glasgow, with Marian Ross born 1832 from the Gorbals, and Francis Ross from the Gorbals born 1852, emigrants aboard the Annie Jane of Liverpool, master William Mason, bound from Liverpool to Quebec, was shipwrecked and drowned near Vatersay in the Outer Hebrides on 28 September 1853. [WAJ]

ROSS, DAVID, born 1817, a shoemaker from Rosskeen in Easter Ross, with Christy Ross, born 1821, and children John Ross born 1845, Isabella Ross born 1848, and Alexander Ross born 1850, emigrants aboard the Annie Jane of Liverpool, master William Mason, bound from Liverpool to Quebec, was shipwrecked and drowned near Vatersay in the Outer Hebrides on 28 September 1853. [WAJ]

ROSS, GEORGE, born 1841, son of William Ross in Philorth, Aberdeenshire, died in San Francisco on 20 July 1890. [Fraserburgh Kirkton gravestone]

ROSS, HUGH, born 1876 in Inverness, son of William Ross [1832-1921] and his wife Isabella Paterson [1837-1902], a carpenter, was drowned in the River Lewis, British Columbia, on 18 June 1898. [Tomnahurich gravestone, Inverness]

ROSS, JOHN, in Pontiac, Illinois, heir to his mother Elspeth Rae, wife of John Rae a labourer in Hightae, Lochmaben, Dumfriesshire, who died on 18 June 1876, on 11 May 1887. [NRS.S/H]

ROSS, THOMAS, of Kingston Grammar School in Upper Canada, a letter to John Lee, Principal of Edinburgh University,7 July 1838. [NLS.ms3439/195-6]

ROSS, Mrs, with master S. Smith, and two maid-servants, emigrated on board the Albion from Aberdeen to Halifax, Nova Scotia in 1829. [NRS.GD316.15.12]

ROWAND, ALEXANDER, MD in Montreal, Quebec, married Margaret Kincaid, daughter of the late Thomas Kincaid a merchant in Leith, in Edinburgh on 25 January 1844. [GM.ns.21.309]

ROY, JAMES, in Windsor, Ontario, an inventory dated 1874. [NRS.SC70.167.887]

RUSSELL, ADAM, in America, an inventory dated 1878. [NRS.SC70.190.294]

RUTHERFORD, H.C., in Dundas, Wentworth, Canada, an inventory dated 1878. [NRS.SC70.189.482]

RUTHERFORD, JOHN MURRAY, from Edinburgh, died at 391 Berkeley Street, Toronto, Ontario, on 19 December 1897. [S.17011]

RUXTON, WILLIAM, son of William Ruxton a merchant in Buffalo in New York, was educated at Marischal College in Aberdeen around 1845. [MCA]

SALMOND, DAVID, in Toronto, Ontario, an inventory dated 1879. [NRS.SC70.196.943]

SALMON, JAMES, on board the SS City of Philadelphia at Chain Cove, Newfoundland, re the grounding of the vessel, a letter dated 13 September 1854. [SRA.TD237]

SANG, DAVID, born 1800, died in New York on 15 October 1842. [St Andrews Cathedral gravestone]

SANGSTER, JAMES, born 1880, son of William Sangster a carpenter in St Fergus, Aberdeenshire, died in Edmonton, Canada, on 3 August 1910. [Crimond gravestone, Aberdeenshire]

SCARTH, JOHN, a from Orkney, later at Hudson Bay, versus John Robertson, a merchant in Stromness, Orkney, in 1803. [OA]

SCOTT, ARCHIBALD, from the Scottish Borders, settled in Canada, a letter to his cousin in Scotland dated about 1845. [NRS.GD1.813.17]

SCOTT, DAVID, in 144 Navy Street, Brooklyn, New York, a sasine dated 6 March 1888. [NRS.R.S.Forfar, Angus, 46/191]

SCOTT, JOHN, settled in Kitchener/Berlin, Ontario, a letter to his uncle in Scotland dated 29 August 1835. [NRS.GD1.813.1]

SCOTT, Dr JOHN, from the Scottish Borders, a physician in Ontario, a letter to his cousin Andrew Redford in Hermiston, Edinburgh, dated 1840. [NRS.GD1.813.4]

SCOTT, JOHN, a mason from Dundee, Angus, later in Philadelphia, Pennsylvania, a sasine dated 6 April 1882. [NRS.R.S.Forfar, Angus. 39/246]

SCOTT, JOHN, a skinner, eldest son of James Scott, a skinner, and nephew of John Nicholl, a skinner in Hawick, Roxburghshire, died in Wansbruck, America. On 11 May 1885. [S.13076]

SCOTT, JOHN, in Duarte, Louisiana, a sasine dated 17 December 1890. [NRS.R.S.Culross, Fife.4/4]

SCOTT, MICHAEL, in Quebec, a letter to his sister Jane Scott in Port Dundas, Canada West, dated 12 February 1849. [SRA]

SCOTT, THOMAS, Chief Justice of Upper Canada, an inventory dated 1873. [NRS.SC70.163.510]

SEATER, JOHN WHITE, of Bonnington Farm, Lothair, Manitoba, eldest son of George S. Seater of Bonnington Farmhouse, Edinburgh, married Bessie Baily, daughter of Zachary Baily, Lothair, in Brandon, Manitoba, on 4 January 1899. [S.17340]

SEIVEWRIGHT, JAMES, son of William Seivewright a merchant in Aberdeen, was educated at Marischal College in Aberdeen around 1848, later minister of the Scots Church in Melbourne, Quebec. [MCA]

SELCRAIG, THOMAS, in Panhandle, Texas, was served heir to his father John Selcraig, a boot and shoemaker in Edinburgh, who died on 4 September 1876. [NRS.S/H]

SERVICE, or TORRANCE, ISABELLA, in Norwich, Connecticut, heir to her father Walter Torrance in Mullany, Currie, Midlothian, who died on 23 April 1848, 14 September 1900. [NRS.S/H]

SHANNON, LIVINGSTON, and Company in Newfoundland, trading with Jamaica, New Providence, New York, Canada, Demerara, and the United States, from 1816 until 1811. [NRS.CS96.905.1; CS233.Seqn., S.1.47]

SHIELD, JAMES ARRAN, son of George Shield the Deputy Clerk of Session, died in Buffalo, New York, on 6 May 1885. [S.13064]

SHIELL, EDITH BEATRICE, youngest daughter of David R. Sheill in Edinburgh, married William Polson, at Dunedin Ranch, Auburn, California, on 7 January 1898. [S.17035]

SILLARS, DONALD, from Maryquil, Arran, aboard the Newfoundland settled in Inverness township, Megantic County, Quebec, in 1831. [TNA.CO384.28.24-26]

SILLARS, DUNCAN, from Monyguil, Arran, settled in Inverness township, Megantic County, Quebec, in 1831. [TNA.CO384.28.24-26]

SILLARS, JOHN, from Maryquil, Arran, settled in Inverness township, Megantic County, Quebec, in 1831. [TNA.CO384.28.24-26]; born 1793, died 22 February 1859. [Inverness, PQ, gravestone]

SILLARS, PETER, with a family of eight persons, from South Sannox, Arran, aboard the Newfoundland bound for Canada, 1829. [TNA.CO384.22.3-5]

SIM, ALEXANDER, son of Alexander Sim a weaver in Aberdeen, was educated at Marischal College in Aberdeen around 1843, later a Congregational minister in Canada. [MCA]

SIMPSON, THOMAS, born in Dingwall, Ross and Cromarty, in 1808, educated at Aberdeen University, settled at Hudson Bay in 1829, died at Turtle River, Canada, on 28 June 1840. [GM.ns.14.548]

SIMPSON, WILLIAM, in USA, a deed in favour of John Simpson's executors, dated 11 November 1865. [NRS.RD1247.527]

SINCLAIR, HENRY, in New York Mills, Oneida County, New York, 31 May 1870, ultimus haeres. [NRS.PS3.16.454]

SINGLETON, Mrs JESSIE, wife of William J. Singleton, died at the residence of her son John Singleton at 311 State Street, Chicago, Illinois, on 9 December 1884. [S.12941]

SKINNER, WILLIAM, in USA, power of attorney to James Stevenson, dated 3 January 1863. [NRS.RD1173.276]

SMALL, EDWARD PATRICK, in Lakeville, California, heir to his father Joseph Small, a pawnbroker in Hamilton, Lanarkshire, who died on 11 February 1888, re property in Hamilton, on 23 July 1889. [NRS.S/H]

SMART, JOHN, born 1860, younger son of William Smart a merchant in Edinburgh, died in Duluth, Minnesota, on 28 November 1884. [S.12928]

SMITH, AGNES BEATRIX, eldest daughter of John W. Smith, died in Tarrytown, New York, on 13 October 1884. [S.12887]

SMITH. Captain ALEXANDER, born 1813, son of Alexander Smith a shoemaker in Aberdeen and his wife Isabella Main, died in New Orleans, Louisiana, on 10 March 1848. [Banchory Ternan gravestone, Aberdeenshire]

SMITH, ANDREW WHYTE, born 1848, died in Toronto, Ontario, on 19 July 1901. [St Andrews Cathedral gravestone, Fife]

SMITH, CHARLES, a joiner from Grantown on Spey, Moray, emigrant aboard the Annie Jane of Liverpool, master William Mason, bound from Liverpool to Quebec, was shipwrecked but survived near Vatersay in the Outer Hebrides on 28 September 1853. [WAJ]

SMITH, DONALD, born on Colonsay, Argyll, emigrated to Prince Edward Island in 1820, died there on 19 March 1875. [Woods Islands Pioneer Cemetery, PEI]

SMITH, DONALD A., emigrated from Forres in 1838, at the North West River, Esquimo Bay, Canada, a letter dated 16 March 1860. [HBCA.PAM.D5/51]

SMITH, or STEPHEN, ELIZABETH, in Roundtop Farm, Randolph County, Illinois, a sasine dated 19 September 1891. [NRS.R.S.Kintore, Aberdeenshire.5.283]

SMITH, GEORGE, in Baxter Springs, Cherokee, Kansas, a sasine dated 19 September 1891. [NRS.R.S.Kintore, Aberdeenshire.5.283]

SMITH, JAMES, son of Alexander Smith, born 1779, died 19 March 1827, a shoemaker in Aberdeen and his wife Isabella Main, settled in Buffalo, New York. [Banchory Ternan gravestone, Aberdeenshire]

SMITH, JAMES, eldest son of Samuel Smith a merchant in New York, matriculated at Glasgow University in 1832, graduated BA in 1835, MA in 1836, and MD in 1837. [RGG]

SMITH, JAMES LAMOND, from Glen Millan, Aberdeen, married Isabella Barker, third daughter of George Barker of Leamington Priory, Warwickshire, in Guelph, Canada, on 22 October 1844. [GM.ns.23.196]

SMITH, JOHN, in Union City, Indiana, a sasine dated 19 September 1891. [NRS.R.S.Kintore, Aberdeenshire, 5.283]

SMITH, JOHN, in Middleton, Wisconsin, heir to his father John Smith, a draper in Portsoy, Banffshire, who died on 21 June 1889, re property there, on 31 March 1900. [NRS.S/H]

SMITH, Mrs MARGARET, in North Parma, New York, an inventory dated 1876. [NRS.SC70.181.449]

SMITH, MARIA FULLERTON, eldest daughter of John Fullerton Smith of Carronhill, Dumfries-shire, married Frank A. Wheeler of Granitestone, De Land, Florida, there on 25 March 1885. [S.13027]

SMITH, MARY DRYDEN, in London, Canada, an inventory, dated 1871. [NRS.SC70.155.260]

SMITH, RANALD, from Skye, Inverness-shire, emigrated via Greenock aboard the *Royal Adelaide* bound for St John, New Brunswick, later to Fredericton, N.B., petitioned the New Brunswick Assembly in 1838. [PANB.RS24.4.77]

SMITH, ROBERT LESLIE, born 1863, son of James Smith and his wife Isabella Walker, died in Providence, Rhode Island, on 21 February 1895. [St Andrews Cathedral gravestone, Fife]

SMITH, WILLIAM, son of William Smith of Glenmillan an advocate in Aberdeen, was educated at Marischal College in Aberdeen around 1848, later of the Standard Assurance Company in Montreal, Quebec. [MCA]

SMITH, WILLIAM GRIFFITH, born 1842, from Edinburgh, died in New York on 15 December 1898. [S.17326]

SMITH, WILLIAM R., in Union City, Indiana, a sasine dated 19 September 1891. [NRS.R.S.Kintore, Aberdeenshire, 5.283]

SOMERVILLE, Reverend JAMES, formerly Professor of Theology at King's College, Fredericton, New Brunswick, died in Brechin, Angus, on 10 September 1852. [GM.ns38.545]

SPENCE, CHARLES, second son of Charles Spence, a Solicitor to the Supreme Court in Edinburgh, died in Goderich, Ontario, on 11 May 1885. [S.13072]

SPRUNT, ALEXANDER, born 28 September 1818 near Perth, emigrated to Wilmington, North Carolina, in 1852, a letter, 1865. [TNA.FO115.444.145/147]

STAUNTON, MOSES, in Toronto, Ontario, an inventory dated 1878. [NRS.SC70.188.104]

STEPHEN, ALEXANDER REID, a farmer in Texas, an inventory dated 1879. [NRS.SC70.193.643]

STEPHEN, ALEXANDER, in Roundtop Farm, Harrisville Randolph County, Illinois, a sasine dated 19 September 1891. [NRS.R.S.Kintore, Aberdeenshire.5.283]

STEPHEN, WILLIAM, a farmer in Texas, an inventory, 1879. [NRS.SC70.197.444]

STEVENSON, ALEXANDER, in Wakopa, Manitoba, was served heir to his father Thomas Stevenson, a printer and bookseller in Kilmarnock, Ayrshire, who died on 27 August 1878. [NRS.S/H]

STEVENSON, PETER, and spouse, in New York, a deed in favour of the survivor, dated 18 May 1860. [NRS.1250.603]

STEWART, ALEXANDER, born 1819, with Rachel Stewart born 1824, Elspet Stewart born 1848, from North Uist, Outer Hebrides, bound via Greenock aboard the <u>Waterhen of London</u> to Quebec in 1849. [NRS.GD221.4435]

STEWART, ALEXANDER, born 1798 in Skye, Inverness-shire, died on Prince Edward Island on 27 February 1890; Catherine, his wife, born 1813 on Skye, died in February 1883. [Little Sands cemetery, PEI]

STEWART, CHARLES, from Forres in Moray, was educated at Marischal College in Aberdeen, later was a merchant in America. [MCA]

STEWART, DONALD, with a family of nine persons, from Margarioch. Arran, bound for Canada, 1829. [TNA.CO384.22.3-5]

STEWART, DONALD, from Arran, emigrated via Lamlash, Arran, aboard the brigantine Caledonia bound for Canada in1829, landed in Quebec on 25 June 1829. [TNA.CO384.28.24/26]

STEWART, DUNCAN, born 1809, with his wife Janet born 1815, and children Catherine born 1841, and John born 1843, from North Uist, Outer Hebrides, emigrated via Greenock aboard the Cashmere of Glasgow bound for Quebec in 1849. [NRS.GD22140l1.53]

STEWART, EDWARD GEORGE, in Selma, Missouri, an inventory dated 1878. [NRS.SC70.187.155]

STEWART, JAMES, from North Kiscadale, Arran, settled in Inverness township, Megantic County, Quebec, in 1831. [TNA.CO384.28.24-26]

STEWART, JAMES CAMPBELL, in Canada, an inventory dated 1878. [NRS.SC70.190.565]

STEWART, JAMES, born 1866, second son of James H. F. Stewart, schoolmaster in Ardross, and his wife Isabella in 1887, and buried in Hamilton cemetery. [Rosemarkie gravestone, Easter Ross]

STEWART, JOHN, eldest son of John Stewart a merchant in Glasgow and Margaret Todd, died in Nashville, Tennessee, on 10 April 1836. [Ramshorn gravestone, Glasgow]

STEWART, JOHN, minister at West Bay, New Brunswick, in 1835, moved to Nova Scotia in 1838. [F.7.608]

STEWART, JOHN, from Skye, Inverness-shire, emigrated via Greenock aboard the Royal Adelaide bound for St John, New Brunswick, later to Fredericton, N.B., petitioned the New Brunswick House of Assembly in 1838. [PANB.RS9924/4/77]

STEWART, JOHN, from Rothesay, Bute, died at Brookhill, Richmond, Virginia, on 12 March 1885. [S.130135]

STEWART, Reverend JOHN, born in 1826, eldest son of Archibald Stewart in Dunamuck, Lochgilphead, Argyll, died in Kincardine, Ontario, on 29 December 1898. [S.17337]

STEWART, KENNETH, born 1839 in Inverness, formerly a miner in Australia and New Zealand, emigrated via Liverpool aboard the Lake Huron in 26 March 1898 bound for Nova Scotia, landed in Halifax, N.S., on 6 April 1898, from there to the Yukon. [TGSI.70.59]

STEWART, MURDOCH, born 1809 in Contin, Ross-shire, graduated MA from King's College, Aberdeen, in 1834, was ordained minister at West Bay, Cape Breton, in 1843, and in Whycocomagh in 1868, died in Pictou, Nova Scotia, on 30 July 1884. [F.7.608]

STEWART, NELLIE EDWARD, in Marshall, Missouri, was served heir to her father Edward George Stewart in Saline County, Missouri, who died on 31 December 1876, re property in New Abbey, Dumfries-shire, [NRS.S/H]

STEWART, ROBERT, from Arran, emigrated via Lamlash, Arran, aboard the brigantine Caledonia bound for Canada in 1829, landed in Quebec on 25 June 1829. [TNA.CO384.28.24/26]

STEWART, RONALD D., born 1827 in Skye, Inverness-shire, died on Prince Edward Island on 15 October 1896. [Little Sands gravestone, P.E.I.]

STEWART, W. L., Captain of the Royal Regiment, son of Lieutenant Colonel Stewart in the Honourable East India Service, married Eliza Saunders Shore, daughter of George Shore of Fredericton, New Brunswick, there on 10 April 1849. [GM.ns.12.84]

STEWART, WILLIAM, born 1768, from Inverkeithing, Fife, died in Stamford, Upper Canada, on 3 July 1838. [GM.ns.10.343]

STIRLING, WALTER, born 3 November 1853, son of Murray Stirling, died on 4 June 1904 in Vernon, British Columbia. [St Andrews Cathedral, Fife]

STIRRAT, MARGARET, wife of George Brown, postmaster at Owen Sound, Canada, ultimus haeres, on 6 October 1855. [NRS.PS3.16.231]

STOBIE, or PULLAR, JANE, in Hamilton, Ontario, heir to her sister Marjory Stobie in St Andrews, Fife, who died on 9 August 1883, on 1 July 1887. [NRS.S/H]

STODDART, THOMAS R., in California, a deed with Reverend P. Maxwell's trustees, dated 3 August 1858. [NRS.RD1062.73]

STOTHART, THOMAS, born 1825, eldest son of John Stothart in Crossbankhead, Dumfries-shire, died in Princeville, Gray County, Canada West, on 17 April 1885. [S.13065]

STOTT, ADELA MAY, born 1875, daughter of Charles C. Stott and grand-daughter of J. H. Stott in Edinburgh, died in Bleping Hospital, Quincy, Illinois, on 26 January 1899. [S.17356]

STRACHAN, ALEXANDER, in St Louis, USA, an inventory dated 1873. [NRS.SC70.160.900]

STRACHAN, FREDERICK, son of William Strachan a merchant in Peterhead, Aberdeenshire, died in Keysville, Harboro, Florida, on 1 July 1884. [S.12808]

STRONG, LAWRENCE, born 1782 in Shetland, a mariner who was naturalised in South Carolina on 27 January 1804. [USNA.M1183/1]

STUART, ALEXANDER, from Inveravon, Banffshire, was educated at King's College in Aberdeen around 1843, later a Congregational minister in Halifax, Nova Scotia. [KCA]

STUART, CHARLES, in Canada West, an inventory dated 1874. [NRS.SC70.167.738]

STUART, WILLIAM, a plumber in Montreal, Quebec, an inventory dated 1871. [NRS.SC70.151.135]

STURROCK, DAVID, in Pennsylvania, letters, from 1837 to 1842. [DUA.ms234/3]

SUTHERLAND, GEORGE SINCLAIR, died in Fond du Lac, Wisconsin, in 1870, a letter to his sister Fanny Sutherland. [NRS.GD139.509]

SUTHERLAND, JAMES, at the Red River Settlement, and Hudson Bay, letters to his brother John Sutherland of Knock Hall, South Ronaldsay, Orkney, between 1814 and 1856. [Orkney Archives.D31]

SUTHERLAND, ROBERT, born 1824 in Caithness, and his wife, born in Caithness, settled in Lochaber, Lower Canada, renamed Thurso, he died in 1908, while his wife died in 1874. [Thurso gravestone]

SWAYNE, THOMAS, in 110 Main Street, Whealing, West Virginia, a sasine dated 5 March 1887. [NRS.R.S.Dysart, Fife.6.208]

TASKER, PATRICK, born 1823 in Greenock, Renfrewshire, settled in St John's, Newfoundland, as an employee of Hunter and Company. [MU.mf313]

TAWSE, WILLIAM, son of William Tawse, born 1767, died 31 October 1858, and his wife Elizabeth McKenzie, born 1779, died 20 January 1848, settled in Guelph, Canada. [Birse gravestone, Aberdeenshire]

TAYLOR, ISABELLA, wife of William Funkie, late of Edinburgh, died in Boston Hylands, USA, on 22 January 1885. [S.12975]

TAYLOR, JOHN, settled in Reach, Ontario, by 1848, a petitioner. [NRS.GD112.61.5]

TAYLOR, JOHN SWANSTON, in Quebec, an inventory dated 1873. [NRS.SC70.161.393]

TEMPLE, ROBERT, son of Robert Emmett [sic] in New York, a student a Marischal College in Aberdeen, graduated MA in 1857. [MCA]

TEMPLETON, JAMES, in Town Dane, USA, an inventory dated 1878. [NRS.SC70.193.301]

THIN, JOHN, in Millford, Manitoba, heir to his mother Isabella Clouston, widow of Robert Thin, a merchant in Liverpool, who died on 18 November 1884, re property in Edinburgh, 5 August 1887. [NRS.S/H]

THIN, ROBERT, in Chicago, Illinois, heir to his mother Isabella Clouston, widow of Robert Thin, a merchant in Liverpool, who died on 18 November 1884, re property in Edinburgh, on 5 August 1887. [NRS.S/H]

THOMSON, COLIN, in Duluth, USA, heir to Elizabeth Ann Falconer, widow of William Dallas a merchant in Inverness, who died on 14 March 1869, re property in Inverness on 25 July 1889. [NRS.S/H]

THOMSON, GEORGE AUGUSTUS, of the Florida Land and Colonization Committee, letter to Sir William MacKinnon dated between 1865 and 1893. [NRS.NRAS.0323]

THOMSON, GEORGE, a Presbyterian minister in Canada, an inventory dated 1871. [NRS.SC70.154.507]

THOMSON, ISABEL BEATRICE, born 1884, daughter of D. M. Thomson, died at Frankfort Station, Will County, Illinois, on 4 February 1885. [S.13000]

THOMSON, JAMES, in Denver, Colorado, heir to his father James Thomson in Aberdeen who died on 23 November 1886, re property in Aberdeen, 23 March 1887. [NRS.S/H]

THOMSON, JAMES S., in Caterville, South Dakota, son of John Thomson a manufacturer in Strathmiglo, Fife, married Mary Beatt Nickerson, daughter of Reverend Norman F. Nickerson, in Britton, Michigan, on 19 January 1898. [S.17041]

THOMSON, MATTHEW, in New York, a will on 14 August 1863. [NRS.RD1248.587]

THOMSON, PATRICK, a baker in Quebec, a deed dated 23 October 1829. [NRS.RD433.189]

THOMSON, WILLIAM, formerly at Hudson Bay, later on South Ronaldsay, Orkney, in 1805. [OA]

THORBURN, Sir ROBERT, born 28 March 1836, settled in St John's, Newfoundland, in 1852, a merchant of the firm Barrie, Johnston, and Company, Prime Minister of Newfoundland and Labrador in 1895, died 12 April 1906. [DCB]

THORNTON, PETER, in Hamilton, Canada a mandate with David Martin, dated 5 October 1857. [NRS.RD.1175.267]

TOLDEROY, JAMES BAILLIE, of Frederickton, New Brunswick, born 1808, graduated MD from Glasgow University in 1830, died on 4 September 1860. [RGG]

TOLMIE, JOANNA, second daughter of James Tolmie in Campbeltown, Argyll, married Montague William Drake, in Victoria, Vancouver Island, on 12 March 1862. [GM.ns.2/13.222]TORRANCE, ARCHIBALD, jr., in Norwich, Connecticut, heir to his father Walter Torrance in Mullany, Currie, Midlothian, who died on 23 April 1848, on 14 September 1900. [NRS.S/H]

TORRANCE, DAVID, was born 1840 in Edinburgh, was Chief Justice of the Supreme Court of Connecticut, died in 1906. [SS.775]

TORRANCE, JOHN, in Norwich, Connecticut, heir to his father Walter Torrance in Mullany, Currie, Midlothian, who died on 23 April 1848, on 14 September 1900. [NRS.S/H]

TOVEY, JOHN, in Quebec, Power of Attorney in favour of John Foreman, dated 12 October 1830. [NRS.RD425.363]

TUCKER, CRAWFORD, and Company, merchants in Newfoundland in 1832. [NRS.CS46.1832.4.68]

TUDHOPE, ARCHIBALD, born 1801, eldest son of Thomas Tudhope Crown a merchant in Paisley, Renfrewshire, matriculated at Glasgow University in 1813, minister in Annan, Dumfries-shire, from 1834 to 1838, then in Philadelphia, Pennsylvania, and elsewhere in the USA, died in Cincinnati, Ohio, on 6 September 1861. [RGG]TURNER, Sir H., in Bermuda, a letter re Lieutenant Hope of the 96th Regiment, dated 30 August 1826. [NRS.GD45.3.581]

UNDERWOOD, FRANCIS HENRY, born in Enfield, Massachusetts, on 12 January 1825, graduated LL.D. from Glasgow University in 1887, died in Edinburgh on 7 August 1894. [RGG]

URQUHART, ALEXANDER, from Skye, Inverness-shire, emigrated via Greenock aboard the Royal Adelaide bound for St John, New Brunswick, later to Fredericton, N.B., petitioned the New Brunswick House of Assembly in 1838. [PANB.RS24/4/77]

USHER, GEORGE, in Hamilton, Wentworth County, Canada, ultimus haeres, on 10 December 1866. [NRS.PS3.16.395]

VAIL, EDWIN A., of America, graduated CM from Glasgow University in 1837. [RGG]

WALKER, ALEXANDER, a fiddler and a gardener at Castle Newe, Aberdeenshire, emigrated to America, settled at Beaverwyck, New York, by 1870. [UA.GB231.ms1018]

WALKER, ALEXANDER, a coal merchant in Jersey City, USA, heir to his father Alexander Walker, a slater in South Muir of Kirriemuir, Angus, who died on 18 February 1900, re property there, on 30 October 1900. [NRS.S/H]

WALKER, ANDREW, late of J. Walker and Company, brewers in Cincinatti, Ohio, died there on 24 July 1884. [S.12817]

WALKER, DAVID A., a butcher from Forfar, Angus, later at Walker's Farm, Northburgh, Worcester County, Massachusetts, a sasine dated 22 August 1893. [NRS.RS.Forfar.53.273]

WALKER, EDWARD, settled in Reach, Ontario, by 1848, a petitioner. [NRS.GD112.61.5]

WALKER, HELEN SMITH, in Brockton, Toronto, heir to her father James Walker, a draper in London, who died on 27 June 1881, re property in Ladybank, Fife. [NRS.S/H]

WALKER, JOHN, a merchant in St John's, New Brunswick, an inventory dated 1871. [NRS.SC70.154.438]

WALKER, MARGARET, daughter of John Walker a leather merchant in St Andrews, Fife, died in New York on 30 August 1849. [FJ]

WALLACE, JAMES, a lithographer in West Saint Louis, USA, heir to his great grandfather William McHoull, a papermaker in Galston, Ayrshire, who died on 5 November 1848, re property in Galston, on 6 June 1889. [NRS.S/H]

WALLACE, JAMES, born 1852, son of John Wallace in Leith, died in Honolulu, Hawaii, on 15 December 1897. [S.17035]

WALLACE, PETER, born 1852, eldest son of Alexander Wallace a draper in Bo'ness, West Lothian, fell overboard from the SS Alaska in Lower Bay, New York, and drowned on 7 June 1884. [S.12787]

WARDROP, RICHARD, in St Louis, Missouri, was served heir to his mother Jessie Whyte Glen or Wardrop in London, who died on 15 March 1886. [NRS.S/H]

WATSON, JAMES, eldest son of the late James Watson a Writer to the Signet in Edinburgh, died in Toronto, Ontario, on 9 April 1845. [GM.ns.24.103]

WALKER, THOMAS, born 1852, son of John Walker in Gordonbush, [1827-1886], and his wife Mary Williamson, [1829-1896], died in Jackson, USA, on 24 May 1893. [Clyne Kirkton gravestone, Sutherland]

WATSON, PETER, a painter in Claremont, New Hampshire, heir to his mother Isabella Purves, widow of James Watson, a hardware merchant in Brechin, Angus, who died on 10 October 1888, re property in Brechin, on 30 April 1889. [NRS.S/H]

WATT, FREDERICK WILLIAM MINNIKEN, in Poughkeepsie, New York, was served heir to his mother Eliza Henry, widow of George Watt in Turriff, Aberdeenshire, who died on 27 February 1891. [NRS.S/H]

WEDDERSPOON, Mrs SARAH GIBB or, in Sharles, San Francisco, California, an inventory dated 1872. [NRS.SC70.160.367]

WEIR, GEORGE, from Aberlour in Banffshire, graduated LLD from King's College in Aberdeen, later a Professor of Classics in Kingston, Quebec. [KCA]

WELSH, WILLIAM, in Watertown, Massachusetts, heir to his brother Thomas Welsh in Edinburgh, who died on 6 January 1900, on 28 September 1900, re property there. [NRS.S/H]

WESTWOOD, CHARLES, at Bennal Heights, Cartland Avenue, San Francisco, California, a sasine dated 24 August 1893. [NRS.R.S.Kirkcaldy, Fife, 28.79]

WESTWOOD, HUGH, a painter in 123 East 54th Street, New York, a sasine, dated 24 August 1893. [NRS.R.S.Kirkcaldy, Fife, 28.79]

WETMORE, THOMAS S., a 'British-American' graduated MD at Glasgow University in 1839. [RGG]

WHITE, ANDREW WATSON, a butcher in Jamestown, New York, heir to his father Charles White a butcher in Edinburgh, who died on 4 January 1883, on 14 February 1900. [NRS.S/H]

WIGELSWORTH, JOHN, in Ontario, an inventory dated 1871. [NRS.SC70.152.804]

WILSON, ADAM, letters re Trafalgar, Upper Canada, dated 1832. [NLS.ms.3439/155-6]

WILSON, AGNES, in Petersburg, Virginia, an inventory dated 1876. [NRS.SC70.181.568]

WILSON, ANDREW, born 1806 in Edinburgh, son of Andrew Wilson, died in Toronto, Ontario, on 18 October 1864. [GM.ns.3.1.141]

WILSON, JAMES, in Holy Cross, Dakota, an inventory dated 1874. [NRS.SC70.169.595]

WILSON, JAMES LEIGH MCDOUGALL, only child of James Reid Wilson and grandson of James Wilson, 4 Craigpark, Denniston, Glasgow, died in Montreal, Quebec, on 14 May 1885. [S.13058]

WILSON, JOHN, born 1800 in Edinburgh, a vocalist, died in Quebec on 8 July 1849. [GM.ns.32.547]

WILSON, JOHN, a joiner in Brooklyn, New York, was served heir to his mother Margaret Ferguson or Wilson in Kilmarnock, Ayrshire, who died on 26 July 1897. [NRS.S/H]

WILSON, MATTHEW, was born on 1 January 1806 in Cadder, Lanarkshire, son of Alexander Wilson a farmer, was educated at Glasgow University, a missionary ordained for Sydney Mines on Cape Breton, died on 13 December 1884. [F.7.608]

WILSON, ROBERT, in Philadelphia, Pennsylvania, an inventory dated 1873. [NRS.SC70.162.419]

WILSON, WILLIAM PRINCE, of America, graduated MD from Edinburgh University in 1826. [EMG]

WILSON, Mrs, in New York, a deed in favour of A. Wilson, dated 18 December 1829. [NRS.RD418.689]

WISHART, ANDREW, in Dunbar, Pennsylvania, her to his grandfather William Sutherland, a carter in Burntisland, Fife who died in January 1846, re property in Largs, Ayrshire, on 26 March 1887. [NRS.S/H]

WOOD, DAVID, a blacksmith in Jersey City, USA, a sasine dated 9 June 1899. [NRS.RS.Dysart, Fife, 10.189]

WOOD, GEORGE, in De Kalb, Illinois, was served heir to his father Robert Wood in Whitecraig, Inverness, who died on 28 April 1846, re property in East Lothian. [NRS.S/H]

WORK, JOHN, a schoolteacher in Sorrento, California, heir to his uncle John Work, a joiner in Kirkwall, Orkney, who died on 18 April 1891, on 4 April 1900. [NRS.S/H]

WOOD, JOHN, an advocate in USA, an inventory dated 1871. [NRS.SC70.151.810]WYLLIE, ALEXANDER, late of Pearce Street, Brechin, Angus, died in the Cedar Forest, Virginia, on 10 January 1899. [S.17344]

WYLLIE, JOHN, a glover in Orleans, Vermont, a sasine dated 1864. [NRS.RS.Whithorn.4.35/43]

WYLLIE, ROBERT CRICHTON, born in Dunlop, Ayrshire, on 13 October 1798, second son of Alexander Wyllie of Hazelbank, the Minister of Foreign Affairs in Hawaii, died in Honolulu on 24 November 1865. [GM.ns3/1.284]

YATES, JAMES, a merchant on Vancouver's Island, British Columbia, a sasine dated 1896. [NRS.RS.Dysart, Fife.9.75]

YOUNG, ANDREW HOUSTON, from Quebec, married Janet Greenshields, second daughter of Thomas Greenshields, in Kilmarnock Ayrshire, on 12 January 1841. [GM.ns.15.200]

YOUNG, ANDREW, a farmer in Red Oak, Michigan, was served heir to his cousin Andrew Young, son of Andrew Young in Galston, Ayrshire, who died on 10 May 1899. [NRS.S/H]

YOUNG, Reverend JOHN, in Greenfield, Iowa was served heir to his father John Young, a labourer in Bathgate, West Lothian, who died on 22 December 1894. [NRS.S/H]

YOUNG, KENNEDY DOUGLAS, born 1817 in Castle Douglas, died in Charleston, South Carolina, in 1840. [Kelton gravestone, Kirkcudbrightshire]

YOUNG, WILLIAM, of America, graduated MD from Glasgow University in 1842. [RGG]

YUILLE, GEORGE, a merchant in Glasgow, trading with Virginia, New York, South Carolina and Louisiana between 1811 and 1819. [NRS.CS96.2227-2234]

ADDENDUM

SCOTTISH SETTLERS TO THE USA AND CANADA BEFORE 18--

ALLAN, ..., son of James Allan, a sailor aboard ships trading between Glasgow and Virginia and South Carolina in 1767. [NRS.GD1.32.38/33]

ANDERSON, ALEXANDER, farmer at Monymusk, Aberdeenshire, was contracted to go from Aberdeenshire via London to East Florida in the service of Sir Archibald Grant of Monymusk, Sir Alexander Grant of Dalvey, and Duncan Grant of Antigua, on 20 June 1767. [NRS.GD1.32.38]

ANDERSON, JAMES, petitioned for land in East Florida in 1767. [NRS.GD1.32.3826]

ARTHUR, ROBERT, master of the Brothers of Greenock trading with Charleston, South Carolina, in 1727. [TNA.CO5.509]

BAIN, ALEXANDER, a merchant in Greenock, trading with New and South Carolina from 1772 until 1783. [NRS.CS96.198]

BALFOUR, ROBERT, master of the Whydah of Greenock was shipwrecked off the coast of South Carolina on 6 January 1803. Charleston Courier.2]

BOG, JAMES, master the St Andrew of Greenock trading with North Carolina in 1771. [NRS of.E504.15.19]

BOG, ROBERT, a merchant in Greenock trading with New York in March 1784. [NRS.AC7.61]

BOGLE, ROBERT, in Shettleston, Glasgow, formerly in Virginia and Maryland, by 1795 trading with Demerara and Tobago. [NRS.CS96.3201]

BOUCHER, JAMES, from Greenock in Renfrewshire, a member of the Scots Charitable Society of Boston, New England, in 1735. [NEHGS]

BRADSHAW, THOMAS, was granted land in East Florida in 1767. [NRS.GD1.32.38.26]

BUCHANAN, GEORGE, a merchant in Greenock, trading with New Brunswck in 1796. [NRS.E504.15.73]

BUCHANAN, HUGH, born 1773 in Greenock, a mariner who was naturalised in South Carolina on 8 May 1805. [NARA.M1183.1]

BUCHANAN, JOHN, born 1726, a merchant in Greenock trading with New York and New Brunswick, in 1796, died on 20 October 1814. [NRS.E504.15.73] [Greenock gravestone]

BURNET, WILLIAM, from Aberdeen, a sailor in Philadelphia, Pennsylvania, in 1793. [NRS.S/H]

CALHOUN, JOHN, and Company, merchants in Glasgow, owners of the Neptune of Glasgow, master James Maxwell, trading in linen and cotton with Boston, New England, in 1728. [NRS.CS96.3814]; bound from Glasgow to Rotterdam to load goods to exchange for slaves on the coast of Guinea, then via Cork to Africa to acquire slaves, gold dust and elephant teeth, then from Guinea to the Leeward Islands or Barbados or Jamaica to dispose of the slaves and to purchase sugar and cotton before returning to Scotland. Captain James Maxwell died off the Coast of Guinea in 1731. [NRS.CS228.A.3.19]

CAMERON, DUGALD, master of the Renown of Greenock trading with Newfoundland in 1796. [NRS.E504.15.72]

CAMERON, WILLIAM, from Greenock, a member of the Scots Charitable Society of Boston, New England, in 1731. [NEHGS]

CAMERON, SAM, a soldier of the 2ND Battalion of the 84th [Royal Highland Emigrants], Regiment on the frigate Raleigh bound from New York to Charleston, South Carolina, in November 1780, an agreement to receive and discharge the prize money due to them subscribed at Charleston on 4 December 1780 [NRS.GD174.2405]

CAMERON, WILLIAM, from Greenock, a member of the Scots Charitable Society of Boston, New England, in 1731. [NEHGS]

CAMPBELL, Lord WILLIAM, petitioned for land in East Florida in 1767. [NRS.GD1.32.38.26]

CARPENTER, SAMUEL, from America, a student at Marischal College in Aberdeen in 1759. [MCA]

CHALMERS, JAMES, from Greenock, a member of the Scots Charitable Society of Boston, New England, in 1757. [NEHGS]

CHALMERS, JAMES, master of the Prince of Wales of Greenock trading with Virginia in 1769. [NRS.E504.15.17]

CAMERON, WILLIAM, from Greenock, a member of the Scots Charitable Society of Boston, New England, in 1731. [NEHGS]

CHALMERS, Mr formerly clerk of Mr Morrison in Leith, now in St Augustine, East Florida proposed as agent there for Sir Archibald Grant in 1773. [?] [NRSGD1.32.38]

CHARLES, CLAUDIUS, a surgeon in Halifax, Nova Scotia, by 1776, in 1777 he was a surgeon at the General Hospital of New Hampshire, in 1783 he returned to Nova Scotia and later to England. [TNA.AO12.102.245]

CHARLES, ROBERT, was granted land in East Florida in 1767. [NRS.GD1.32.38.26]

CHISHOLM, JOHN, master of the Lady Jane of Pittenweem in Fife, to Hampton in Virginia on 4 June 1766; master of the Countess Kelly of Pittenweem to Norfolk, Virginia, via Amsterdam in Holland in April 1768, arrived in Anstruther from Hampton, Virginia, on 9 November 1768. [NRS.E504.3.3/4]

CLERK, JAMES, master of the Katie of Greenock trading with Virginia in 1774. [NRS.E504.24]

CLERK, JOHN, a boy aboard the Cathcart bound for the Chesapeake in 1724. [NRS.AC9.1712]

CLERK, JOHN, master of the Alexander and Ann of Aberdeen returned to Aberdeen from Virginia in October 1751. [AJ]

COCHRAN, JOHN, a cotton yard merchant in Glasgow, trading with Honduras, Mexico, and New York between 1828 and 1831. [NRS.CS96.690.1/2]

COCHRANE, THOMAS, master of the Mally of Greenock trading with North Carolina in 1774. [NRS.E504.15.24]

COCHRANE, WILLIAM, master of the Speedwell of Greenock trading with North Carolina in 1784. [NRS.E504.15.39]

COOPER, Captain, master of the St Andrew of Aberdeen trading between Aberdeen, Montrose, and Virginia from 1751 until1752. [AJ]

CRAIG, BARBARA, divorced John Caldwell in New England later married John Fisher in Burnside of Dundonald, Ayrshire, between 1723 and 1730. [NRS.CH1.2.62.41-51]

CRAWFORD, JAMES, aboard the Cathcart bound for the Chesapeake in 1724. [NRS.AC9.1712]

CRAWFORD, MALCOLM, master of the Ritchie of Greenock trading with South Carolina and Virginia between 1766 and 1769. [NRS.E504.15.17/18]

CRISP, JAMES, was granted land in East Florida in 1767. [NRS.GD1.32.38.26]

CUMMINS, WALTER, Controller of St Augustine, was granted land in East Florida in 1767. [NRS.GD1.32.38.26]

CUNNINGHAM, PHILIP. took the Association Oath in New York on 14 May 1696. [TNA]

CUNNINGHAM, ROBERT, master of the Ajax of Greenock trading with North Carolina from 1774 to 1775. [NRS.E504.15.23]

DENISTOUN, JOHN, master of the British Queen of Greenock trading with Charleston, South Carolina, from 1788 until 1790. [NRS.E504.15.48/50/56]

DONALD, WILLIAM, a merchant in Greenock trading with America in 1781. [NRS.AC9.3032]

DUNBAR, JOHN, master of the St Andrew of Aberdeen trading between Virginia and Montrose in Angus in March 1757. [NRS.CE53.1.4]

DUNCAN, ARCHIBALD, a merchant in Glasgow, trading with Mexico, Cuba, Haiti, Columbia, Montreal, and New York, in 1830. [NRS.CS96.912.1]

DUNDAS, ALEXANDER, from Greenock, a member of the Scots Charitable Society of Boston, New England, in 1747. [NEHGS]

ELLIOT, WILLIAM, was granted land in East Florida in 1767. [NRS.GD1.32.38.26]

ELMSLIE, Captain, master of the St Andrew from Aberdeen bound for Virginia in August 1752. [AJ]

ESON, ROBERT, master of the Jeannie of Greenock trading with South Carolina in 1769. [NRS.E504.15.17]

FACHRIE, JAMES, born 1773 in Greenock, died in Savanna, Georgia on 17 July 1809. [Savanna Death Register]

FARQUHARSON, JOHN, a letter from Charlestown, South Carolina, dated 11 May 1771 to Sir Archibald Grant of Monymusk re possible plantations in Georgia and South Carolina. [NRS.GD1.32.38]

FAUNTLEROY, GEORGE, from America, a student at Marischal College in Aberdeen in 1760. [MCA]

FAUNTLEROY, MOORE, from America, a student at Marischal College in Aberdeen in 1760. [MCA]

FELLOWS, NATHANIEL, master of the Speedwell of Greenock trading with Boston, Massachusetts, in 1766. [NRS.E504.15.13]

FINNEY, ANDREW, from Greenock, a member of the Scots Charitable Society of Boston, New England, in 1732. [NEHGS]

FLECK, WILLIAM, master of the Sisters of Greenock trading with Newfoundland in 1791, also master of the Sally of Greenock trading with Newfoundland in 1792. [NRS.E504.15.59]

FLUCKER, HANNAH, daughter of the deceased Thomas Flucker, late of Boston, New England, now residing in Edinburgh, was married in Boston in November 1776, a Process of Divorce against her husband James Urquhart, formerly Major of the 14th Regiment of Foot, in January 1787. [NRS.CC8.6.777]

FRASER, DONALD, a soldier of the 2ND Battalion of the 84th [Royal Highland Emigrants], Regiment on the frigate Raleigh bound from New York to Charleston in November 1780, an agreement to receive and discharge the prize money due to them subscribed at Charleston on 4 December 1780. [NRS.GD174.2405]

FRASER, JAMES, born 1759 in Greenock, died in Darien, Georgia, on 18 December 1828. [Georgia Republican, 29.12.1828]

GEDDES, JOHN, took the Association Oath in New York on 14 May 1696. [TNA]

GEDDES, GEORGE, master of the Gordon of Kerston, arrived in Anstruther in Fife from New York on 26 May 1766. [NRS.E504.3.4]

GERARD, WILLIAM, in New York, a contract with Juan Albarez Vesina, a shipmaster, to ship a cargo from New York to the Caribbean in May 1782. [NRS.GD1.768.13]

GLAISTER, ROBERT, born 1771 in Greenock, died in Savanna, Georgia on 8 October 1806. [Savanna Death Register]

GORDON, Lieutenant ADAM, was granted land in East Florida in 1767. [NRS.GD1.32.38.26]

GORDON, JOHN, a mariner on the St Andrew of Aberdeen, arrived in Montrose, Angus, from Virginia in April 1757. [NRS.CE53.1.4]

GORDON, Captain, of the Ruby of Aberdeen trading between Aberdeen and Virginia in 1750-1751. [AJ]

GRAHAM, EDWARD, took the Association Oath in New York on 14 May 1696. [TNA]

GRAHAM, JAMES, the Recorder, took the Association Oath in New York in New York on 14 May 1696. [TNA]

GRANT, DAVID, from America, a student at Marischal College in Aberdeen in 1759. [MCA]; graduated MD from King's College in Aberdeen in 1764. [KCA]

GRANT, DONALD, a soldier of the 2ND Battalion of the 84th [Royal Highland Emigrants], Regiment on the frigate Raleigh bound from New York to Charleston in November 1780, an agreement to receive and discharge the prize money due to them subscribed at Charleston on 4 December 1780. [NRS.GD174.2405]

GRANT, J., a letter to Sir Alexander Grant re Jamaica and Dr Stork's ship in East Florida, dated15 November 1769. [NRS.GD1.32.38]

GRANT, Dr WALTER, estimates of settling a plantation in East Florida, dated in May 1767. [NRS.GD1.32.38]

GREGORY, JAMES, was aboard the Cathcart bound for Maryland and Virginia in 1724. [NRS.AC9.1712]

GREIG, ARCHIBALD, master of the Montrose of Aberdeen arrived in Montrose, Angus, in September 1758 from Virginia. [NRS.CE53.1.4]

GREIR, JOHN, was granted land in East Florida in 1767. [NRS.GD1.32.38.26]

GROVER, JOHN, was granted land in East Florida in 1767. [NRS.GD1.32.38.26]

GROVER, WILLIAM, Chief Justice of East Florida, was granted land in East Florida in 1767. [NRS.GD1.32.38.26]

GUILLIS, Captain, master of the Unity of Greenock trading with Newfoundland in 1792. [NRS.E504.15.68]

GUTHRIE, JAMES, the Assistant Quarter Master General in Jeremie, Haiti, from 1796 until 1798, later from 1799 to 1801 a Brigade Major in Canada. [NRS.GD188.28.1]

GUTHRIE, JOHN, master of the Ritchie of Greenock trading with New York and Florida in 1777. [NRS.E504.15.27]

HAMILTON of BARGANY, JOHN, was granted land in East Florida in 1767. [NRS.GD1.32.38]

HARRIS, RUSSEL, from America, graduated MA from Marischal College in Aberdeen around 1765. [MCA]

HARTLEY, RICHARD, master of the Potomac Merchant of Montrose arrived in Port South Potomac, Virginia on 6 July 1752.

HARVEY, JOHN, a soldier of the 2ND Battalion of the 84th [Royal Highland Emigrants], Regiment on the frigate Raleigh bound from New York to Charleston in November 1780, an agreement to receive and discharge the prize money due to them, subscribed at Charleston on 4 December 1780. [NRS.GD174.2405]

HERVIE, Captain, master of the Caledonia of Aberdeen arrived in Aberdeen from Virginia in February 1752. [AJ]

HONEYMAN, JAMES, son of James Honeyman minister at Kinneff in Kincardineshire, a student at Marischal College in Aberdeen, graduated MA in 1764, later a minister in Newport, Rhode Island. [MCA]

HUNTER, ANDREW, a merchant in Leith, trading with New York and Jamaica from 1774 until 1777, a letter-book. [NRS.CS96.1986]

HUTTON, Captain ALEXANDER, and Edward Burd, supercargo of the Christian bound from Leith to Newfoundland in 1727 to load a cargo of fish for sale in Barcelona in Spain. [NRS.RH15.54.4/6]

JACKSON, THOMAS, a soldier of the 2ND Battalion of the 84th [Royal Highland Emigrants], Regiment on the frigate Raleigh bound from New York to Charleston in November 1780, an agreement to receive and discharge the prize money due to them subscribed at Charleston on 4 December 1780. [NRS.GD174.2405]

JACKSON, WILLIAM, was granted land in East Florida in 1767. [NRS.GD1.32.38.26]

JAMIESON, DAVID, took the Association Oath in New York on 26 May 1696. [TNA]

JOHNSTON, JAMES, petitioned for land in East Florida in 1767. [NRS.GD1.32.38.26]

JONES, ARTHUR, Controller of East Florida, was granted land in East Florida in 1767. [NRS.GD1.32.38.26]

KINLOCH, FRANCIS, was granted land in East Florida in 1767. [NRS.GD1.32.38.26]

KNOX, WILLIAM, Agent for East Florida, was granted land in East Florida in 1767. [NRS.GD1.32.38.26]

LEA, ALEXANDER, master of the Ann of Glasgow arrived in Anstruther in Fife on 6 November 1765 from Virginia. [NRS.CE04.3.3]

LEES JOHN, the former barrack-master of Newfoundland in 1794. [NRS.GD51.6.137/253]

LICKLY, Captain, master of the Leathly of Aberdeen trading between Aberdeen and Maryland in 1751 and with Virginia in 1752. [AJ]

LINDSAY, Sir JOHN, petitioned for land in East Florida in 1767. [NRS.GD1.32.38.26]

LORIMER, W., in Albany, New York, a letter to Mr Grant dated 20 May 1758. [NRS.GD248.177.1]

LOW, JOHN, was born 1754 in Scotland, a runaway indentured servant of John Tate a wheelwright in Lurgan township, Cumberland County, Pennsylvania, in July 1774. [PaGaz.2384]

MCCLURE, ALEXANDER, a merchant in St John's, Newfoundland, in 1783. [NRS.CS228.B.6.67]

MCDONALD, DONALD, a soldier of the 2ND Battalion of the 84th [Royal Highland Emigrants], Regiment on the frigate Raleigh bound from New York to Charleston in November 1780, an agreement to receive and discharge the prize money due to them subscribed at Charleston on 4 December 1780. [NRS.GD174.2405]

MCDONELL, DUNCAN, a shopkeeper in St Thomas parish, Quebec, a memorial dated 1786. [TNA.AO13.80.293-297]

MCDOUGALD, ALEXANDER, a soldier of the 2ND Battalion of the 84th [Royal Highland Emigrants], Regiment on the frigate Raleigh bound from New York to Charleston in November 1780, an agreement to receive and discharge the prize money due to them subscribed at Charleston on 4 December 1780. [NRS.GD174.2405]

MCDOUGALD, ANDREW, a soldier of the 2ND Battalion of the 84th [Royal Highland Emigrants], Regiment on the frigate Raleigh bound from New York to Charleston in November 1780, an agreement to receive and discharge the prize money due to them subscribed at Charleston on 4 December 1780. [NRS.GD174.2405]

MCFARQUHAR, COLIN, student at Marischal College in Aberdeen around 1750, later minister at Applecross in Pennsylvania. [MCA]

MACHRY, …., a mariner aboard the St Andrew of Aberdeen from Virginia to Montrose in Angus in 1757. [NRS.CE53.1.4]

MACKAY, FRANCIS, in Montreal, formerly Surveyor of Woods in Canada, later a Lieutenant of the 75th Regiment, a memorial in 1778. [TNA.AO]

MCKENZIE, WILLIAM, a piper in Captain Peter Campbell of Glenure's Company, a letter with American regimental news, dated 7 February 1778. [NRS.GD170.3158]

MCKENZIE, WILLIAM, a cabinet maker in Quebec by 1775. [TNA.AO13.81.274-277]

MCKNIGHT and MCILWRAITH, haberdashers in Ayr, trading with John McDonald and Company, merchant in Montreal, Quebec, in 1798. [NRS.CS9.608]

MACLAINE. ARCHIBALD, of Lochbuy, a soldier in North America, letters from 1776 until1779, and from 1780 to 1781. [NRS.GD174.1307/1316/1349]

MACLAINE, Captain MURDOCH, in Halifax, Nova Scotia, a letter dated 2 September 1782. [NRS.GD174.1349]

MACLAINE, MURDOCH, a soldier of the 2ND Battalion of the 84th [Royal Highland Emigrants, Regiment on the frigate Raleigh bound from New York to Charleston in November 1780, an agreement to receive and discharge the prize money due to them subscribed at Charleston on 4 December 1780. [NRS.GD174.2405]

MCLEAN, HECTOR, a soldier of the 2ND Battalion of the 84th [Royal Highland Emigrants], Regiment on the frigate Raleigh bound from New York to Charleston in November 1780, an agreement to receive and discharge the prize money due to them subscribed at Charleston on 4 December 1780. [NRS.GD174.2405]

MCMILLAN, WILLIAM, a soldier of the 2ND Battalion of the 84th [Royal Highland Emigrants], Regiment on the frigate Raleigh bound from New York to Charleston in November 1780, an agreement to receive and discharge the prize money due to them subscribed at Charleston on 4 December 1780. [NRS.GD174.2405]

MCNIVEN, JAMES, a fisherman in Nova Scotia, later at New Carlisle, Bay of Chaleur, New Brunswick, in 1786. [TNA.AO13.81.182.281]

MCQUEEN, PETER, a soldier of the 2ND Battalion of the 84th [Royal Highland Emigrants], Regiment on the frigate Raleigh bound from New York to Charleston in November 1780, an agreement to receive and discharge the prize money due to them subscribed at Charleston on 4 December 1780 [NRS.GD174.2405]

MARTIN, JOHN, a mariner aboard the St Andrew of Aberdeen arrived in Montrose, Angus, on 18 April 1757 from Virginia. [NRS.CE53.1.4]

MASON, KENDER, was granted land in East Florida in 1767. [NRS.GD1.32.38.26]

MELVIN, ..., master of the Adventure of Aberdeen trading between Aberdeen and Virginia in 1751. [AJ]

MONTGOMERY, ALEXANDER, petitioned for land in East Florida in 1767. [NRS.GD1.32.38.26]

MONTGOMERY, JAMES, was granted land in Queen's County Nova Scotia, by Lord W. Campbell the Governor of Nova Scotia on 31 December 1768. [NRS.CH12.12.1125]

MORRISON, JAMES, petitioned for land in East Forida in 1767. [NRS.GD1.32.38.26]

MUDIE, ROBERT, master of the Thomas and Betty of Montrose trading with Virginia in 1747 and 1749. [NRS.CE53.1.2/4]

MURRAY, Admiral, a letter from Halifax, Nova Scotia, dated 7 November 1795. [NRS.D24.1.402]

NICOLL, W., took the Association Oath in New York on 26 May 1696. [TNA]

OCHTERLONIE, GEORGE, master of the Rebecca and Mary of Montrose, arrived in Montrose on 22 February 1735 from the Potomac River in Virginia. [NRS.CE53.1.2]

OSWALD, RICHARD, was granted land in East Florida in 1767. [NRS.GD1.32.38]

PARKER, CHARLES STEWART, born 1771, son of a Scottish merchant, in Norfolk, Virginia, an apprentice in Grenada from 1789, a partner in Sandbach, Tinne and Company in 1792, married Margaret Rainy or Creich, died in 1828. [RSSP.116]

PEARSON, GEORGE, master of the Mary of Montrose from Montrose in Angus to Charleston in South Carolina and return via Rotterdam in 1770. [NRS.CE53.1.7]

PEDDIE, ANDREW, master of the Elizabeth trading between Dundee and Edenton in North Carolina, in 1774-1775. [NRS..CE70.1.6]

PEEBLES, JOHN, a letter regarding the recapture of St John's, Newfoundland, by Lieutenant Colonel Amherst, dated 20 September 1762. [NRS.GD21.487]

PENMAN, JAMES, was granted land in East Florida in 1767. [NRS.GD1.32.38.26]

POPHAM, ALEXANDER, was granted land in East Florida in 1767. [NRS.GD1.32.38.26]

PRIDE, MARGARET, in Pittsburgh, Pennsylvania, only daughter of James Pride the younger, a candlemaker in Leslie, Fife, and his wife Betty Webster, a deed 20 July 1797. [NRS.B65.4.1,436-441]

RAMSAY, JAMES, a student at Marischal College in Aberdeen, around 1750, son of George Ramsay a physician in Virginia. [MCA]

RAY, FRANCIS, born 1723, absconded from the snow Elizabeth of Aberdeen in New York in June 1741. [Zenger's New York Weekly Journal, 29 June 1741]

REA, JAMES, master of the Minerva of Dundee from Dundee to Charleston, South Carolina, in April 1765, [NRS.CE70.1.4], arrived there in August 1765. [South Carolina Gazette, 28.8.1765]

REID, ALEXANDER, master of the Friendship of Anstruther in Fife, arrived in Anstruther from Virginia on 14 May 1766. [NRS.E504.3.4]

REID, JOHN, a merchant in Carolina, son of John Reid a shipmaster in Cromarty, 1771. [NRS.CS16.1.143]

ROBERTSON, Lieutenant Colonel JAMES, was granted land in East Florida in 1767. [NRS.GD1.32.38.26]

ROBERTSON, General JAMES, Governor of New York, Letterbook 1780-1783. [NRS.GD172/2599]; Barrack Master papers, 1765-1776. [NRS.GD172.2624]

ROSE, DAVID, a shipmaster from Inverness and a landowner in Craven County, South Carolina, in 1743. [SCSA. S.C. Deeds Abstracts, 1719-1772, vol.2, fo.72]

ROSS, ROBERT, born in Aberdeen, settled as a merchant in Pensacola, West Florida, in 1764, moved to the Mississippi as a merchant and planter in 1772, moved to Halifax, Nova Scotia, by 1785. [TNA.AO13.26.414-423]

SHEDDEN, WILLIAM, in Bermuda and New York, letters, from 1780 until 1784. [NRS.GD1.67.1]

SINCLAIR, JAMES, an army officer in St Pierre, Martinique, letters to Alexander Bower of Kincaldrum in Angus, in 1796. [NRS.GD503.151]

SINCLAIR, ROBERT, born 1659 in Kirkwall, Orkney Islands, a mariner in New York by 1680. [TNA.HCA.Vol.81]

SINCLAIR, ROBERT, took the Association Oath in New York on 14 May 1696. [TNA]

SMITH, JOHN, master of the 105 ton ship Jean of Ely in Fife, from Anstruther in Fife to Charleston in South Carolina in November 1768, returned to Anstruther on 2 June 1769, also on 27 April 1770. [NRS.E504.3.3]

SPALDING, JAMES, a merchant in East Florida and Georgia, a sasine 1772. [NRS.RS.201.215]

SPENCE, JAMES, master of the Marjory Packet of Montrose, arrived in Montrose in Angus on 12 October 1731 from Virginia. [NRS.CE53.1.2]

SPINK, JOHN, master of the Concord of Arbroath in Angus, arrived in Arbroath on 25 November 1740 from Port Hampton in Virginia. [NRS.CE53.1.5]

SPITAL, JOHN, in Fort St Lawrence, Nova Scotia, a letter concerning military life there, dated 6 December 1750. [NRS.GD172163]

SQUYRE, JOHN, in Charlestown and in Boston, a letter to the Presbytery of Edinburgh in 1715. [NRS.CH1.2.35.189-194]

STOBO, ARCHIBALD, in Boston, New England, a letter to the Presbytery of Edinburgh in 1715. [NRS.CH1.2.35.189-194]

STUART, JOHN, Superintendent of East Florida, was granted land in East Florida in 1767. [NRS.GD1.32.38.26]

SWAN, MICHAEL, a soldier of the 2ND Battalion of the 84th [Royal Highland Emigrants], Regiment on the frigate Raleigh bound from New York to Charleston in November 1780, an agreement to receive and discharge the prize money due to them subscribed at Charleston on 4 December 1780. [NRS.GD174.2405]

TAIT, JAMES, from Orkney, a mariner on board HMS Captain died in Boston, Massachusetts, probate 1774, Prerogative Court of Canterbury. [TNA]

TAYLOR, ABRAHAM, a shipmaster from Aberdeen, later a ships chandler in Boston, Massachusetts by 1753. [NRS.CS16.1.192]

TAYLOR, ALEXANDER, late of Charleston, South Carolina, later in Calton Hill, Edinburgh, sasines 1776 to 1778, NRS.RS.229.231; 240.121/125/254; 241.248.]

TAYLOR, JAMES, was granted land in East Florida in 1767. [NRS.GD1.32.38.26]

TAYLOR, WILLIAM, Colonel of the 9th Regiment, was granted land in East Florida in 1767. [NRS.GD1.32.38.26]

THOMSON, ANDREW, took the Association Oath in New York on 14 May 1696. [TNA]

THOMSON, PETER, master of the Fanny and Betty of Aberdeen trading between Aberdeen and Virginia in 1752, also between the James River, Virginia, and Montrose in Angus in 1757. [AJ]

THOMSON, Captain, master of the Ann of Aberdeen trading between Aberdeen and Virginia in 1750, 1751, and 1752. [AJ]

THORNTON, THOMAS, was granted land in East Florida in 1767. [NRS.GD1.32.38.26]

THORNTON, WILLIAM, master of the Fame from Dundee via Madeira to Cape Fear in North Carolina, and Charleston, South Carolina, in February 1773. [NRS.CE70.1.6]

TOWNSEND, THOMAS, was granted land in East Florida in 1767. [NRS.GD1.32.38.26]

TURNBULL, Dr ANDREW, Clerk of the Crown, was granted land in East Florida in 1767. [NRS.GD1.32.38.26]

UDNEY, GEORGE, was granted land in East Florida in 1767. [NRS.GD1.32.38.26]

WATSON, JOHN, the younger, formerly a planter in Maryland and Virginia, a merchant in Edinburgh, trading with Martinique, Pennsylvania, Barbados and Jamaica, between 1696 and 1713. [NRS]

WELCH, WILLIAM, took the Association Oath in New York on 14 May 1696. [TNA]

WHYTE, JOHN, master of the Happy Betty of Kirkcaldy in Fife, arrived in Anstruther in Fife from Virginia on 26 May 1766. [NRS.E504.3.4]

WILSON, ..., a mariner aboard the St Andrew of Aberdeen from Virginia to Aberdeen in April 1757. [NRS.CE53.1.4]

WOOLRIDGE, THOMAS, Provost Marshal of East Florida, was granted land in East Florida in 1767. [NRS.GD1.32.38.26]

www.ingramcontent.com/pod-product-compliance
Lightning Source LLC
Chambersburg PA
CBHW070334230426
43663CB00011B/2317